Behind the
Japanese mask...

If you want to know how...

The Arab Way
How to work more effectively with Arab cultures

Working with the Americans
*How to work and communicate
successfully with Americans in business*

The Chinese Business Puzzle
How to work more effectively with Chinese cultures

Brilliant Business Connections
How to build professional relationships and make them work

howtobooks

Send for a free copy of the latest catalogue to:

How To Books
3 Newtec Place, Magdalen Road,
Oxford OX4 1RE, United Kingdom
email: info@howtobooks.co.uk
http://www.howtobooks.co.uk

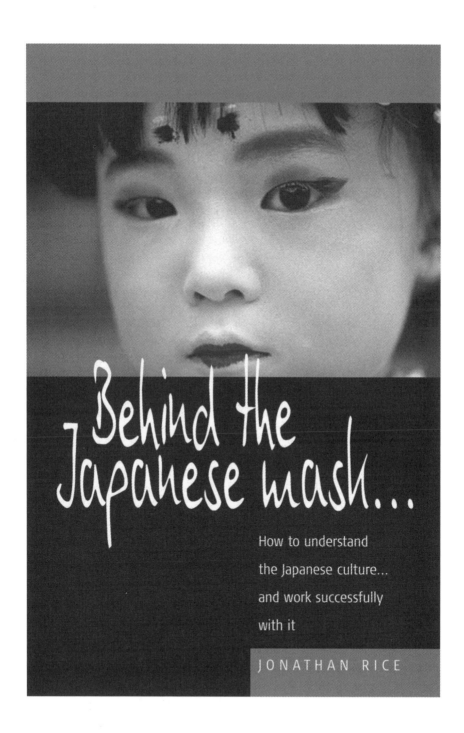

Behind the Japanese mask...

How to understand
the Japanese culture...
and work successfully
with it

JONATHAN RICE

howtobooks

Published by How To Books Ltd,
3 Newtec Place, Magdalen Road,
Oxford OX4 1RE. United Kingdom.
Tel: (01865) 793806. Fax: (01865) 248780.
email: info@howtobooks.co.uk
http://www.howtobooks.co.uk

British Library Cataloguing in Publication Data
A catalogue record for this book is available from the British Library

Cover design by Baseline Arts Ltd, Oxford
Produced for How To Books by Deer Park Productions, Tavistock, Devon
Typeset by PDQ Typesetting, Newcastle-under-Lyme, Staffs.
Printed and bound by Bell & Bain Ltd., Glasgow

NOTE: The material contained in this book is set out in good faith for general guidance and no liability
can be accepted for loss or expense incurred as a result of relying in particular circumstances on
statements made in the book. The laws and regulations are complex and liable to change, and readers
should check the current position with the relevant authorities before making personal arrangements.

Contents

Preface

'It is with no little trepidation that I have ventured to enlist myself in the large army of those who have written about Japan.' These were the first words of the preface to *In Lotus Land Japan*, written by the British photographer and diarist Herbert Ponting in 1910. Almost a century on, I can only echo Mr. Ponting's words. However, I would put forward as my excuse the fact that Japan is still – even after the torrent of words written and broadcast in the century and a half since the country first subjected itself to Western ways – persistently misunderstood. If this book can persuade a few people to look at Japan in a different light, and to try to consider its people and its culture without any preconceived Western ideas or values getting in the way, then perhaps the effort in writing it will have been worth it.

Japan is an enigma. Everybody seems to feel that there is something mysterious about Japan. As another early visitor to Japan, Augusta Campbell Davidson, wrote in 1907, 'the much talked of Europeanisation of Japan has been, as it were, a mechanical rather than a chemical process. The two streams, where they co-exist at all, seem to flow side by side like oil and wine: each remains distinct. The new may overlay and even hide the old, but that which lies beneath persists undiminished, practically unchanged.' As she noted, 'Within a stone's throw of the big foreign hotel, there is a Buddhist temple.' There still is.

But consider the position of a Japanese coming to Europe for the first time. He or she could just as easily write, 'Within a stone's throw of the big hotel, there is a Christian cathedral.' These days there will also be a Japanese restaurant, several curry houses, a kebab takeaway and any number of examples of American culture. All around the world, there is a veneer of international cultural, and of globally accepted values and norms, but under the surface the different cultures still assert their differences – and quite rightly too.

Nobody can learn or know everything about a culture, even about their own culture. Nor should we assume that the Japanese culture, or any other culture, is uniform. Everybody will have their own impressions of what is important about the country and its people. However, in writing this book, I have tried to steer the reader towards the main issues that make Japan different from anywhere else in the world, so that their experiences of Japan may be even more enjoyable. I have made no attempt to cover every aspect of Japanese life, nor to come up with an answer to every confusing situation a foreigner may ever encounter.

A little learning is a dangerous thing, but only if you think you have learnt everything. Japan is endlessly fascinating, and endlessly worth learning about.

Jonathan Rice

About the Author

Jonathan Rice first visited Japan as a child, spending a year in Tokyo at the age of eight. He read Japanese at Cambridge University, and then lived and worked in Japan for a dozen years. During that time he set up and managed the Japanese subsidiary of a leading British electronics and engineering company, and negotiated licences, joint ventures and import/export deals with Japanese partners. He sat on the board of a Japan/UK joint venture company for 12 years, during which time they achieved a 75% market share in their range of medical products. He still visits Japan regularly.

He set up his own consultancy business in 1990, specialising in national and organisational culture. He advises firms on marketing strategies overseas as well as on strategies for change and growth in the UK. He also works on all aspects of organisational and cultural change; cultural due diligence before and after mergers; and effective in-house communication styles and techniques for multinational companies. He is the creator of the *Favourite Words* cultural diagnostic device which has proved successful with many clients in identifying cultural differences and clashes across different cultures and different parts of an organisation.

Jonathan Rice is a regular speaker at Farnham Castle, and has run seminars for them and other clients in many different countries around the world. He is the author of over 50 books.

Farnham Castle International Briefing and Conference Centre

A lack of cultural understanding and local practices can be a major obstacle to the effectiveness of conducting business in another country. The ability to relate quickly and effectively with colleagues and clients in a new country is very important to long term success.

Farnham Castle International Briefing and Conference Centre is widely acknowledged as the world's leading provider of intercultural management training and briefing and has an unmatched reputation for helping individuals, partners and their families to prepare to live and work effectively anywhere in the world.

Through its unrivalled faculty of trainers and experts, Farnham Castle offers a totally flexible and comprehensive range of programmes providing the first-hand knowledge and skills required to be successful in international business including:

- workshops on developing cross-cultural awareness
- working effectively with specific cultures or nationalities
- cross cultural communication, presentation and negotiation skills training
- country and business briefings for any country in the world
- intensive tuition in any language.

Full details available on website at: www.farnhamcastle.com

1

The Japanese Mask

Japan is a strange country. It is such a strange country that the Japanese even think that Europeans and Americans are strange, and how foolish is that! For most Westerners, Japan is little more than a country a long way away, where they speak a bizarre and unintelligible language and where the word 'inscrutable' was probably invented. They make many things that we in the West use and need, from Toyota and Honda cars to Seiko watches, from Canon copiers to Minolta cameras, from Sony Walkmen to Toshiba laptops. But when they sell us their goods, they tend to come over to our country and speak more or less fluent English, so why should we bother to learn more about their country, their customs and their way of doing business? If the Western rules of international behaviour and of doing business are dominant in the world – and they are – then are we not merely in danger of piling confusion upon misunderstanding by trying to learn more about the way they do things at home?

Well, if the nearest you want to get to Japan is to buy a Walkman or drive your Lexus around the streets of your home town, then perhaps you are right, and this book is not for you. However, if you have any business relationship with the Japanese, whether as customer, supplier, partner or competitor, then it certainly helps to have a better grasp of their society and culture, as well as their business practices.

WHY CAN'T THEY BE MORE LIKE US?

The Japanese have never been easy to understand. What is more, they hardly ever try to be understood. For Western people, used to expressing our emotions and opinions clearly, Japanese reserve and inscrutability is not only impossible to work out, it is also very irritating. Why can't they be more like us? Why do they hide their feelings and their opinions so deftly and why do they not go about their business and their lives in the straightforward way that Europeans and Americans do?

Digital and analogue

This commonly stated view begs the question of whether the Japanese sit in equal bafflement at the strange ways of the West: they do, but for them the question is more likely to be, 'Why can't we be more like them?', which takes us to the heart of the Japanese character. As one Japanese colleague explained it to me, Westerners are digital but the Japanese are analogue. Whereas Western people are individuals, who have intrinsic merit of their own and who do not feel the need to define themselves in terms of other people, Japanese can only operate as part of a larger system, like one hand on the face of an analogue clock, only of value when in a relationship with somebody or something else.

Ask a Brit, for example, 'Who is that person over there?' and he will reply, 'She is my sister.' In reply to the same question, a Japanese would say, 'I am her brother.' The end result is the same – we know who that person over there is – but for the Briton, he is at the centre of the world, and the person over there is defined in terms of the speaker. If there was nobody over there, the Westerner would still have a value, in his eyes at least. The Japanese response implies that the person over there is at the centre of the relationship, and that the speaker only has a definition in terms of this other person. Take them away, and how is the Japanese going to define himself? Take away the hour hand, and how can the minute hand tell the time by itself?

IS IT WORTH TRYING TO UNDERSTAND THEM?

One very successful British businessman, who ran a thriving trading house in Tokyo for many years, claimed to have made no attempt whatsoever to understand his hosts. He concluded early in his stay in Japan that they were from another planet, a very friendly planet it must be admitted but a different planet all the same. He used to boast that he had learnt only two words of Japanese in the 20 years he had lived there. The first word was *urusai*, which means 'troublesome' or 'a nuisance', which he would shout at full volume across his office or into the street below if something got on his nerves. The second word was *mizuwari*, which means 'whisky and water', his panacea against all the *urusai* things that he came up against in his daily life.

He maintained that with these two expressions, his grasp of the useful words in the Japanese vocabulary was complete and that to learn too much about the Japanese was counter-productive: they all knew from their first glimpse of him that he was a foreigner, so the Japanese would modify their behaviour to deal with him. If he modified his Western behaviour too much when dealing with the Japanese, there was a grave danger of the two sides overcompensating for each other, which would merely cause even greater confusion and mistrust than was there already. He would argue that his success in selling imported goods to the Japanese proved his theory.

This theory works in practice only if you do not wish to build a strong relationship with your Japanese contacts, and if you have something so desirable for them to buy that they will in any case beat a path to your door. Most of us, however, in dealing with Japan or any other alien business culture, do not have this better mousetrap which will allow us to shout '*urusai*' and call for a *mizuwari* when times get tough. Most of us have to take a few hesitant steps in the direction of the other culture if we are to succeed in establishing a relationship. And relationships, as we shall see, are at the core of conducting business successfully with the Japanese.

UCHI AND *SOTO* – INSIDERS AND OUTSIDERS

Japanese culture is unique. It must be, because the Japanese keep on telling us so. On the other hand, all cultures are a little different from each other, so all cultures must be unique. It's just that the Japanese culture is more 'unique' than the rest. Its uniqueness lies in the clear distinction it has made historically between insiders and outsiders, between the *soto* and the *uchi*. *Soto* means 'outside' in Japanese; *uchi* means 'inside'.

The homogeneity of the Japanese race over 2,000 years or more has created a society in which the difference between its members and those who are mere visitors has become vast – not just in looks and etiquette but in ways of thinking and acting as well. What is more, the Japanese distinguish between *soto* and *uchi* in their behaviour towards the different groups. They act towards foreigners in a way in which they would not behave with fellow Japanese, and when they are overseas, they happily do things they would never think of doing at home.

With those who are *uchi* the Japanese will disclose their deepest secrets, but with those who are *soto*, the best you can hope for is a kind of benign neglect. Total politeness and civility at all times, of course, will be the hallmark of their behaviour, but there is no chance they will talk about things that are dear to their hearts, unless the weather or the local restaurants are what turns them on.

The Japanese mask their feelings in dealing with each other, just as they do in dealing with outsiders. Not all Japanese are as *uchi* as each other, and degrees of separation are carefully maintained within Japanese society just as they are with outsiders. You have only to watch the Japanese *sarariman* on a train in the rush hour, all elbows and shoving for a seat in exact duplication of his Western counterpart, to see that on public transport, everybody is *soto*. Once they reach their offices, they are back *uchi* and they treat their colleagues as insiders. It is not a matter of friendship, it is a matter of relationship. Office colleagues are insiders, whether they like each other or not. Personal feelings are irrelevant, because anybody within the same group, the same family, company or school, is inside and all insiders are treated equally. True feelings are carefully masked.

THE VIRTUE OF MASKING TRUE FEELINGS

The mask is a common feature of Japanese culture, from the Noh and Kabuki dramas to folk songs and even children's television, where one of the best loved adventure series of the past 30 years was called *Kamen Raida*, which means 'Masked Rider'. It is pointless to expect Japan and the Japanese to be easily interpreted by outsiders when the masking of true feelings and intentions is, and always has been, such a virtue in Japan.

Looking for the truth behind the words

In all areas of Japanese life, but especially in business negotiations, the Japanese make use of *tatemae* and *hon-ne*. *Tatemae* is usually translated as 'the official position' and is what will be expressed in words. The *hon-ne* or 'true voice' is unlikely ever to be heard out loud, although the Japanese themselves can understand it from the range of emotions and expressions used in stating the official position. The art of being able to hear the true voice of Japanese feelings is one that is not easily acquired, but at least if you are aware that all Japanese expect there to be a difference between what is said and what is meant, then you will learn to look for the truths between the words, rather than the simple facts that the words may convey. This is yet another mask of Japanese feelings and intentions, which can be very confusing for a newcomer to their way of doing things. However, you have to remember that this is not a show they put on especially for the foreigners or other people who are, for one reason or another, *soto*. It is the way they conduct themselves even within their most intimate circles: it is their natural way of doing things.

THE CHANGING FACE OF JAPAN

Perhaps at this stage, before we have become too dogmatic in our statements of how all Japanese do everything, we should note that Japan is changing. Japan has always been changing, even in the feudal period when the *status quo* was meant to be preserved absolutely and change was proscribed by law. However, in the latter years of the twentieth century and the early years of the twenty-first, there is little doubt that the changes that are taking place in Japanese society are significant and accelerating.

The influence of post-war hardship and poverty

There is a huge difference in attitude between the younger

generation, those under about 45 years of age, and the older generation. The older Japanese remember the post-war years of hardship and poverty, when the aim of everybody was to have enough money to buy a Parker pen for the office and an air-conditioning unit for the apartment; when the most important thing was to have a job, any job, which would bring in an income; and when the art of saving for harder times was firmly established. The impact of the Second World War on Japanese society was total – they entered the 1950s with a new constitution, a recently undeified Emperor and a country in ruins. Those who lived through those years, and appreciated the achievement of the nation's material aims, have a very different attitude towards life, work and the family than those who are too young to remember the difficult days, except through the memories of their parents and grandparents.

The younger Japanese are more sophisticated than their parents, they are less acquisitive because they already have everything, and they are far more influenced by the rest of the world, encountered on television, in the movies and in real life, than the Japanese who were educated before the war or in the early post-war years.

But some things remain unchanged

However, it is also true that in many ways Japan is not changing. There are certain rules and habits of Japanese society that do not change because economic conditions vary, or because McDonald's and Pizza Hut are as widely available in Japan as noodles and sashimi. Japan is still a foreign country. A former resident of Japan, who returned for the first time in over 20 years in 2003, remarked that it was amazing how much had not changed, both physically and in the manners and customs of the Japanese, in two decades, rather than how much had changed. 'I had the feeling I could get straight back into Tokyo life even after all this time,' she said.

Different impressions

We should also notice at this early stage that everybody's impression of Japan is a different one. Although the Japanese love to start their sentences with the phrase 'We Japanese', as though the views and understandings of every one of the 125 million occupants of the islands of Japan are exactly the same, this is self-evidently not so. But for foreigners, coming from the outside and remaining on the outside even though they are doing their best to experience Japan, the impressions of Japan are bound to be a very mixed bag.

A colleague of mine, who worked for several years in Japan, mentioned that he found it very interesting that all Japanese placed such importance on what blood group a person has. He said that the Japanese consider blood group to be a very good way of judging character, and that Type A people are different (in what ways I forget) from Type AB people. This remark sparked a lively debate because in 20 years of living and working with the Japanese, I had never come across this particular habit of 'all Japanese'. However, my assertion that all Japanese insist on wearing exactly the right uniform for whatever activity they are involved in, drew equal reservations from him. He cited several instances of inappropriately dressed golfers, and of hikers on Mount Fuji suffering from exposure and even death because they were not taking even the most basic of precautions against the weather.

The truth of both matters is that a lot of Japanese try to look the part whatever they are doing, whether it is cycling in the full Tour de France kit or wearing company uniforms at work; many Japanese also believe that a person's character can be told by the blood group, but neither habit is something that all Japanese involve themselves in all of the time. My colleague came across the blood group idea very shortly after he arrived in Japan, so it stuck with him. I appeared on a tennis court in Japan within the first few weeks of arriving there, and was greeted on court by people who looked to have flown in straight from Wimbledon. The fact that they were no better players than me (in brown shorts, trainers and an old T-shirt) made me believe that appearances are important to all Japanese, even if the substance is not there. We were both wrong in applying the particular to the general view of Japan – a sin, I must add, that many Japanese are also guilty of.

An abundance of writings on Japan

What is more, there is something about Japan that makes foreigners want to pontificate about it (and this book is, I suppose, merely adding to the weight of pontifications) in print and in the broadcast media as often as possible. There are people who have made a career out of *not* knowing about Japan, as though this strange country and its people will yield its secrets more readily to the untutored eye than to the so-called expert. Books used to have titles like *Too Far East Too Long* or *A Lifetime In Japan*, but now the trend is towards *Instant Japanese* and *Glimpses of Japan*. Soon, no doubt, somebody will be rushing into print with *My 45 Minutes in Transit at Narita Airport*, or producing a television programme about Japan as they overfly Kyushu at night. Although most of these books and programmes have some merit, they frequently give quite different opinions, and quite different answers to the same questions, so the truth is hard to discern.

THE TRUTH BEHIND THE MASK

But what is the truth about Japan? Is it the modern Tokyo, with the modern skyscrapers of Shinjuku and Roppongi, or is it the Yasukuni Shrine, where the war dead are remembered? Is it Mount Fuji or the *Shinkansen* bullet train? Is it Honda and National Panasonic and Casio or is it the Gion district of Kyoto where the *geisha* can still be seeing scurrying to their evening engagements? Is it the schoolchildren in their quaint sailor suits or the sharply dressed *yakuza*, the only surviving wearers of spats in the modern world? Is it the ferro-concrete Osaka Castle, rebuilt after the war, or the tiny wooden redoubt of Inuyama, dating back over 400 years to the days when the civil wars were at their most vicious? Is it a Sony Playstation or sumo wrestling? How can we reconcile the beauty and peace of *ikebana* flower arrangements with the turbulent pace of modern city life in Japan? Which of these is the Japanese mask and which is the true face?

The answer is that all these aspects of Japan are the mask, and they are all also the true face of Japan. Sometimes the mask is the true face, and sometimes it is just a mask.

2

The Japanese Archipelago

THE GEOGRAPHY OF JAPAN

Japan is an island country. This basic geographic fact has shaped
their history and the character of their peoples, and is central to the
way they think of themselves. The Japanese islands stretch across
the north-western corner of the Pacific Ocean, from the
northernmost island, the island of Etorofu which is still occupied
by the Russians 60 years after the end of the Second World War, to
Yonaguni Island off the coast of Taiwan in the south. All in all
there are well over one thousand islands making up the Japanese
archipelago, but over 95% of the land area of Japan is made up of
just four islands, the four main islands by which Japan is identified.
These are called Hokkaido, Honshu, Kyushu and Shikoku.

The entire country is further south than most Europeans imagine:
the northern tip of Japan is roughly on the latitude of Bordeaux,
and the southern reaches of the Ryukyu islands stretch to within
the tropics. Tokyo is on the same latitude as Los Angeles, or
Cairo or Teheran. The rough range of Japan from north to south
equates with the Eastern seaboard of the United States, and much
of the climate that Japan lives through can be compared with the
Atlantic coastline of America – cold winters, hot summers and
regular batterings from strong winds in the late summer and early
autumn. Japan has the further physical disadvantage, shared by
the West Coast of the United States but not by the Eastern
seaboard, of being a very volcanic country, full of geysers and hot
springs, and prone to earthquakes.

VOLCANOES AND EARTHQUAKES

The volcanoes and earthquakes of Japan are not merely exotic features of a distant land. They are real and active and play an important part in defining how Japanese people live.

Active volcanoes

Late in 2003, there was concern that Mount Fuji, which had lain dormant since 1707, was showing signs of renewed activity. An eruption by the largest mountain in Japan (3,776 metres high) would have a devastating effect on Tokyo and the surrounding Kanto plain. There are several active volcanoes in Japan, especially down in Kyushu where Mount Aso, and Sakurajima which erupted violently in 1914, are all active. Showa-Shinzan ('the New Mountain of the Showa Era') in Hokkaido was formed between 1943 and 1945 as a result of volcanic activity near Mount Usu. By September 1945, it had reached a height of 408 metres, and it is still rumbling.

Volcanic activity has also created many hot springs all around Japan, where for centuries people have gone to bathe in the naturally heated pools and streams. They still attract millions of visitors each year.

Devastating earthquakes

The more sinister side of this instability of the earth's crust shows itself in earthquakes. There are earthquakes every day in Japan, some which cannot be felt and some of which can be devastating. For people unused to them, a first experience of an earthquake can be daunting. The vast majority of earthquakes are so slight as to be unnoticeable, and even those which you can feel are usually so mild that the sensation is no more than that of being on a slow-moving train. However, major earthquakes can and do occur, and this fact has made a significant difference to the way the Japanese live.

Building to withstand earthquakes

Traditional Japanese houses tend to be made of wood. This is not just because it is easiest to build in wood, or that trees are one of the few plentiful natural resources in Japan. It is also because if an earthquake strikes, they will collapse with less chance of causing cataclysmic damage. They can also easily be rebuilt. In the twentieth century, the importation of modern technology was constrained by the need for it to be earthquake proof. Even today, practically all electric cables are suspended overhead rather than buried underground as they would be in most western countries, because of the danger of disruption by an earthquake.

The American architect Frank Lloyd Wright also had a huge influence on the way buildings are constructed in modern Japan. In 1921 his Imperial Hotel in Tokyo was completed, and in 1923 a huge earthquake struck. Most wooden buildings collapsed, and those that did not were consumed by the fire that followed the earthquake; but the Imperial Hotel survived. Lloyd Wright had built it of ferro-concrete and based it on a foundation of mud, which allowed the building to sway a little with the earthquake but took the violence out of the tremors. The lessons were quickly learned and since then virtually all new buildings over a certain size have been made of ferro-concrete, using the principles established by Frank Lloyd Wright.

This has not exempted Japan from earthquake damage, as the severe Hanshin earthquake of 1994, which struck Kobe and Osaka, showed only too clearly. However, Japanese anti-earthquake technology is far in advance of most other parts of the world, and their public buildings are far more likely to withstand an earthquake than those in other parts of the world, even in those places like California where earthquakes are a real risk.

Mountainous islands

The country is so seismic because the origins of the Japanese islands are comparatively recent in geological terms. The generally accepted theory is that they were created by the collision of four tectonic plates – the Pacific plate, the Philippine plate, the Amurian plate and the Sea of Okhotsk plate. This has created a country that is mountainous, with the coastline falling quickly away to deep ocean beds, which make coastal navigation much more dangerous than around Great Britain and northern Europe, for example.

The spine of Japan is very mountainous and runs with short, fast flowing rivers, so much so that barely 20% of the whole country is habitable. The total area, some 378,000 square kilometres, is about half as much again as the area of the United Kingdom, but in terms of habitable area, it is barely half the size of habitable Britain.

HOKKAIDO

Hokkaido, the northern island, is the second largest in area of Japan's islands at around 83,500 square kilometres, but is only the third largest in terms of population.

Climate

The climate of Hokkaido, and its main city Sapporo, is sub-Arctic, with deep snow throughout the winter months. The coldest temperature ever recorded in Japan, minus 41 degrees Celsius, was recorded in Asahikawa in Hokkaido. The annual Snow Festival in

Sapporo in February attracts thousands of visitors from all over Japan and elsewhere, and features massive ice carvings, which remain frozen for weeks on end. The Winter Olympics were held there in 1972, but Sapporo remains probably best known within Japan for the local beer company and its main brand, which is also called Sapporo.

The summers in Hokkaido are milder than further south, with average June temperatures around 15 degrees Celsius, several degrees cooler than in Tokyo, and over ten degrees cooler than Kyushu. They are also drier, because Hokkaido is beyond the northern edge of the monsoon belt, which just stretches far enough north to include Tokyo and the Kanto plain on which it lies, but peters out in northern Honshu.

Population and cities

Despite the increasing popularity of winter sports holidays in Hokkaido, and the growth of its agricultural industry – the only part of Japan where agriculture is not based on rice – the island remains underpopulated. Apart from Sapporo itself, with a population of around one million, there is only Otaru, the port for Sapporo, facing the Japan Sea and acting as a stepping off point for the ferries to Russia and Korea, and Hakodate, the town which faces the north coast of Honshu across the Tsugaru Straits, which would classify itself as much more than a small town in Japanese terms.

Sapporo is a new city, having grown from virtually nothing at the end of the nineteenth century. It is laid out in a rectangular grid pattern, but this is not in accordance with the ancient Chinese model, as the ancient capital Kyoto is. It is a copy of the

American grid system. The terrain of Hokkaido is less dominated by steep mountains and fast-flowing rivers (although it is certainly mountainous) than its more sourtherly neighbours. The impression it leaves on the visitor is one of space and openness, at least in comparison with the rest of Japan.

SHIKOKU

The two main southern islands, Shikoku and Kyushu, are very different. Shikoku, the smallest and least populated of the four main Japanese islands, was until quite recently seen as a pleasant agricultural part of the country, left behind by much of what went on in the rest of Japan. It is less than one quarter the size of Hokkaido and about two-fifths of Kyushu's size, or in European terms, a little smaller than Wales. It used to be difficult to reach from Honshu, except by boat across the Inland Sea, but the building of the Seto Ohashi bridge via the stepping stones of small islands in the Inland Sea has made Shikoku more accessible. The England football team, for example, used Shikoku as a their training and hotel base during the 2002 World Cup, although the nearest they actually played was across the bridge in Osaka.

KYUSHU

Kyushu, the southernmost of the main islands, is half the size of Hokkaido, but only one-fifth the size of Honshu. It contains several major cities – Nagasaki, Kita-Kyushu, Fukuoka and Kagoshima, for example – and has for many years been a centre of heavy industry, especially shipbuilding. It is also virtually subtropical at the southern end, and Kagoshima with its sandy beaches, soft palm trees and the permanent veil of smoke over the cone of the Sakurajima volcano, is one of the most popular tourist destinations within Japan.

It must be admitted that the Japanese, like the British, have rather lost their taste for holidaying at home, and prefer to travel just as cheaply to Hawaii or the West Coast of America, or to New Zealand or Europe, but those jaded Tokyoites who stay in Japan and visit Kagoshima can have just as exotic a holiday as those who travel to Honolulu, which is these days almost more Japanese than Japan.

HONSHU

Honshu is the main island where all the main cities are – Tokyo, Osaka, Nagoya, Kyoto, Kobe, Yokohama, Hiroshima and many others. It is as mountainous as the other islands, with only a few coastal plains where the population can maintain a fragile foothold on the land.

Population

The Kanto Plain, which supports Tokyo, Yokohama, Kawasaki, Chiba and other smaller cities spreading mainly north and west from Tokyo, is one of the most densely populated regions in the world. At least 30 million people crowd into an area barely 10,000 square kilometres in area, a population density over ten times that of the United Kingdom. This sense of crowding is nothing new. Even in the eighteenth century, Tokyo (then called Edo) had a population of almost one million, making it one of the largest cities in the world at that time.

Cities

The narrow coastal strip along the southern edge of Honshu, stretching for about six hundred kilometres from Tokyo and Yokohama, via Hamamatsu, Nagoya, Osaka, Kobe and Hiroshima down to Shimonoseki at the tip of Honshu and just across the narrow straits from Kyushu, is where the bulk of Honshu's population live. There are cities which face the Japan Sea coast, such as Niigata, and other conurbations in the northern half of Honshu, such as Sendai and Aomori, but the economic, social and political power of Japan looks south from Tokyo rather than north.

A journey by the *Shinkansen* bullet train from Tokyo westwards will show you a landscape that is built up practically all the way. In the distance you will see mountains, including the awe-inspiring sight of Japan's highest peak, Mount Fuji, but all along the tracks are houses, factories and roads. Almost 80% of Japanese people, according to the latest census, live in administrative cities (or *shi*) which have a population of over 30,000. I used to live in Ashiya, between Kobe and Osaka, and I thought of it as not much more than a village. But it was officially *Ashiya-shi*, a city of more than 30,000 people. The Japanese live in a very crowded world.

OKINAWA AND OTHER ISLANDS

There are other islands in the Japanese archipelago that should not be forgotten. Okinawa is the fifth largest island of Japan, and forms part of the Ryukyu Islands well south of Kyushu. The Ryukyus were only returned to Japan by the Americans in 1972, after a quarter of a century of post-war American rule. The Ryukyus were for many centuries a separate kingdom, even if they broadly acknowledged the hegemony of the Japanese, and the culture is subtly different from the rest of Japan. It is still among the poorest parts of Japan.

Sado Island, in the Japan Sea off the coast of Honshu, is the sixth largest of the Japanese islands, but is less than 1,000 square kilometres in size. It is renowned as a beautiful island in Japanese legend and song, but is now little more than a pretty outpost of Japanese culture in the cold and inhospitable Japan Sea.

The islands of Iki and Tsushima, in the straits between Japan and the Korean peninsula, have been the subject of disputes over the centuries, and Tanegashima, just south of Kyushu, owes its fame to the fact that this is where the first Europeans landed when they came to conquer or convert (whichever was the easier) in the sixteenth century. It says much for Western civilization that the word *tanegashima* has come to mean a blunderbuss or firearm in Japanese – the thing that the Japanese most associated with the new arrivals.

AN ISLAND COUNTRY

So Japan is an island country, one that for most of its recorded history was remote from the mainland of Asia. It may be only a couple of hundred kilometres away, but the seas are deep and rough and the Japanese have historically not been a naval race. Their geographical isolation created a nation that sees itself as homogeneous and different from its near neighbours. It sees its history as being separate from the history of its neighbours and it sees its culture as different – clearly influenced by Chinese culture and in turn presenting influences of its own to Chinese culture – but nevertheless individual and unique in world and regional terms. 'We Japanese' – the phrase that is often used to begin an explanation of how things are done in Japan – is to a great extent justifiable. Japan is physically different from its neighbours and the Japanese do things differently.

THE CLIMATE OF JAPAN

The Japanese climate has always played an essential role in shaping the Japanese way of life and character. It is not just the prevalence of earthquakes, volcanoes and other such evidence of seismic activity that has given them a sense of fatalism which pervades much of what they do: there is also the predictability of the climate which gives them intense pleasure when the predictions come true, and causes difficulties when the unexpected happens.

Monsoon

Japan is on the northern edge of the monsoon belt, as we have seen, and this means not only that the rains are predictable enough and the climate is warm and humid enough for rice to be grown, but also that every autumn, the country may well be lashed by violent typhoons. The English word 'typhoon' derives from the Japanese *taifu* meaning 'a great wind'.

The monsoon climate means that Japan can forecast its weather with a considerable degree of accuracy, at least for the most populous part of the country that is within the monsoon belt. They know they will have dry winters, with only a small chance of snow in the cities to the south of the central mountains. They know they will have brief, rather wet springs, when the temperature increases quite quickly in the space of a few short weeks, and they know there will be a rainy season from early May to late June which is vital for a successful rice harvest. They also know they can rely on hot and very humid summers from the end of the rains until the typhoon season comes around in mid-September to blow the summer heat away, and make way for a very pleasant autumn season.

Cherry blossom time

A feature of the Japanese spring is the brief cherry blossom season. Throughout Japan there are millions of cherry trees (*sakura*) which bloom all too briefly between March and May. The cherry blossom is a symbol of the beauty and fragility of life and many songs and poems have been written in praise of what the Japanese see as something both to look forward to and to regret. Many cherry trees are planted in graveyards, which have thus become a very popular place to hold *hanami* (blossom-viewing) parties, at which people sit underneath the falling blossoms and drink and sing mournful songs of the evanescence of life. The media do their best to help, by treating the blossom as a weather front, or some would say as an advancing army. They publish daily bulletins of where the blossoms have got to in their progress from the south, and give estimates of the best days for viewing the blossoms before they fade and die.

It has to be said that the blossoms in full view by the side of a river or in the gardens of a shrine, or indeed in any of the countless cemeteries of Japan, are a beautiful sight, never to be forgotten by anybody who has been lucky enough to spend time just enjoying their splendour. In recent years, the march of the blossoms has been significantly earlier than usual (up to ten days early in 2003, for example) and the Japanese are worried that global warming will mean that their favoured weekends for viewing the cherry blossom will have to be put forward in future.

The rainy season

At the end of spring, the temperature and humidity rises throughout the country, and by early June, the rainy season, *baiu* in Japanese, comes to Kyushu and works its way northwards and eastwards over the next six weeks or so. There can be very heavy and damaging rainfalls during the rainy season, causing landslides and flooding in less well protected areas, but there is usually very little inconvenience felt in the cities, apart from the need to carry an umbrella everywhere. As the rains fade away, the long hot summer settles in, known more for its intense humidity than for the heat of the sun. The temperature can indeed rise to the high 30s Celsius, but it is the humidity that the visitor will feel. Despite the air-conditioning systems which go at full blast in homes, offices, trains, cars and taxis, in summer you still feel the heat and the stickiness, and many businessmen bring a second or even a third shirt to the office in the morning, to change into as the day wears on. People tend to avoid visiting Japan during July and August, even though these months are not so obviously devoted to holidaymaking as they are in Europe and North America.

The *Bon* Festival

In Japan, the main holiday festival in the summer is the *Bon* Festival (also known as *o-bon*) in mid-July, when the spirits of the dead are supposed to return to their native villages. It has a firm basis in Buddhist teaching, and is a fascinating mixture of the solemn and the high-spirited, as so many Japanese events are. The purpose of the festival is to honour the memory of the dead and to 'stimulate ancestor-worship and filial piety', in the words of one authority.

In actual fact it involves people going back to the villages or towns that their family originally came from, to greet the souls of their dead ancestors. Greeting the souls of one's dead ancestors is obviously a joyful occasion, so mixed in with the filial piety and ancestor worship are big meals, parties and dancing. The *Bon Odori* (Bon dance) is still performed in many villages as a community dance in which hundreds of people will take part, dancing throughout the night to a rhythmic clapping of hands and beating of drums.

The autumn typhoon season

The summer eventually gives way to autumn, and brings in the typhoon season. Most of the typhoons which blow across the northern and western Pacific do not reach Japan: the severest typhoons each year tend to hit Taiwan, the Philippines and the Chinese mainland. However, they can be extremely destructive even as far north as the Japanese coast. The Ise Bay typhoon in late September 1959, for example, killed about 5,000 people in the Nagoya area.

When to visit

The best times for visiting Japan are the spring, during the cherry blossom season, and in the post-typhoon early winter, from mid-October until the end of the year. Japan's humidity means that it has never been a popular destination for beach and sun holidays, although there are plenty of beaches around the country that attract local holidaymakers.

For business, there is no time of year which should obviously be avoided, with the one exception of 'Golden Week', a period from 29 April to 5 May when there are three national holidays and, usually, a weekend as well. Everybody goes away on holiday during those ten days or so, and no business visitor should set up a trip to Japan then. There will be nobody to do business with if you do.

THE MYTHOLOGY OF JAPAN

The relationship between the Japanese people and their homeland can best be summed up in the myth of the creation of Japan. According to the earliest Japanese legends, which were originally handed down by oral tradition and were not written down until about the eighth century AD, the islands of Japan were created by the gods Izanami and Izanagi. The pair became husband and wife and in due course Izanagi, no doubt very painfully, gave birth to the islands of Japan. At this point, they decided to create somebody to rule the land, and gave birth to the Sun Goddess, Amaterasu. Among the other children they produced was the evil Storm God, Susa-no-o.

Susa-no-o was banished from the heaven that his parents had created for his various acts of wickedness, but he nevertheless managed to be involved in the creation of the Japanese Imperial line. The myth tells us that the child who went on to found the Imperial line was actually created in the mouth of Susa-no-o, but only after he had chewed up his sister Amaterasu's holy ornaments. She therefore claimed that the child was hers as much as her brother's. According to the original nineteenth century translation of the myth,'the august name of the Deity that was born from the jewels that were twisted on her right august arm, and having crunchingly crunched them, he blew them away, was His-Wondrous-Augustness-of-Kumanu'.

The imperial family

His-Wondrous-Augustness-of-Kumanu in due course reproduced and it was his line that became the imperial family of Japan. The first Emperor, Jimmu, who is supposed to have become Emperor in 660 BC, is traditionally taken to be His-Wondrous-Augustness-of-Kumanu's grandson. The present emperor, Akihito, is 125th in an unbroken line from Jimmu. It was not until the present emperor's father, Hirohito, renounced his divinity in 1945, that the emperors of Japan were considered to be mere mortals.

A close connection with the land

The legend, while obviously no more than a simple myth, shows the connection between the Japanese people and their country. According to this legend, both the emperor and the country he reigns over are descended from the same line. The first emperor, Jimmu, was practically a first cousin to the land he ruled. The relationship between the people and their country could not be closer. A Japanese cannot imagine himself to be Japanese unless he is part of his homeland, and equally, a foreigner cannot become truly Japanese because he is not part of the family which includes the land as well as its people. It is hard to find another example of the close – one might almost call it intense – relationship between the Japanese people and their country. Perhaps the way the Jewish people identify with Israel, their Holy Land, is the only parallel.

JAPANESE RELIGION

The Japanese are not what we in the West would think of as a religious race. Their lives are broadly unaffected by religious beliefs, and their moral codes are based on philosophical rather than spiritual ideas. Nevertheless, religion plays a role in Japanese society, and like everything else about the archipelago, is peculiarly Japanese.

SHINTO

The mythology of the birth of Japan is part of what is now known as *Shinto*, which translates as 'The Way of the Gods'. As one

Japanese authority has put it, 'Viewed from a purely scientific viewpoint, "primitive Shinto" is nothing but an underdeveloped, childish set of religious beliefs. Emotionally, however, "primitive Shinto" is regarded as a pure vitally important religion by the Japanese.' It is interesting that the Japanese themselves can see that to an outsider the ideas of Shinto might be considered childish, yet at the same time they would consider them pure and vitally important. As somebody once described it to me, 'I believe it, but I know it isn't true.' In the West, we may pride ourselves on a more sophisticated concept of religion, but even the most erudite Biblical or Talmudic scholar would understand that simplicity is a virtue rather than a disadvantage in philosophical terms.

Gods of the natural world

Shinto is based around the concept of *kami*, which translates as 'god'. In Shinto, the gods are everywhere, in a tree, a mountain or a waterfall. They are not humanised beings with a physical shape for people to worship; they are the essence of the tree or the mountain or the waterfall. They are not really there to help human beings except inasmuch as they reflect humanity's relationship with the natural world. Mount Fuji is not a god, and nor do the gods dwell on Mount Fuji in the way that the ancient Greeks believed their gods lived on Mount Olympus. The essence of Mount Fuji, its significance to the Japanese, is the *kami*.

Kami helpers

There are other *kami* who might be seen as the equivalent of the Christian patron saints, who help different types of people. Fishermen, woodcutters and swordmakers, for example, would all revere *kami* who do not so much protect them as provide them with the skills they need to achieve greatness in their chosen field. Then there are the *kami* who protect one family or village. All *kami* expect that the people they oversee will make the effort to help themselves. It is not enough for a man to pray to a *kami* to make him a great hunter or farmer – he must also put a great deal of effort into improving himself and thus achieving his aims. The *kami* is there to bring reward for these efforts rather than to replace them. Not for nothing are effort and persistence prime virtues in Japan.

Shinto shrines

Shinto shrines are everywhere in Japan. During the early part of the twentieth century, as nationalism and militarism took a hold over Japanese society, there was an attempt to formalise state Shinto around the figure of the Emperor, and the idea that Shinto could in some way be compared to state religions like, for example, the Church of England or the Russian and Greek Orthodox churches, was promulgated. But Shinto has never been based around a series of frequent and regular visits to holy places, as Christianity, Judaism or Islam require, and it would be wrong to suggest that Shinto was ever organised to that extent.

All the same, Shinto shrines are regularly visited at certain times of the year – on New Year's Day, for example – or on special occasions such as for weddings or coming-of-age ceremonies. Visit any one of the major shrines at any time and you will see very many people offering a little money and saying a brief prayer.

Shinto has a part to play in Japanese life, but the outsider tends not to notice because it is not a determined proselytising religion seeking converts. In fact, it is very much the opposite: Shinto is the religion for Japan, and is not relevant to outsiders. That is one reason why the Japanese do not feel it is anybody else's business but their own if the prime minister or any other government official chooses to visit the Yasukuni Shrine in Tokyo, which is sacred to the memory of those who died in war. The list of people enshrined there includes several who were executed for war crimes after 1945, and outsiders might therefore consider official visits by Japanese politicians to Yasukuni as insensitive at best.

BUDDHISM

The other main religion of Japan is Buddhism, and the two coexist very easily. Buddhism came over to Japan in the latter part of the sixth century AD, from China and Korea. The monks who brought the new religion also brought with them sutras written in Chinese, the first writing that Japan had ever seen. For this reason as much as any other, the impact of Buddhism was immediate and very great.

Buddhism is inherently very different from Shinto, as it looks for the evils of the world within men's desires and to purity of the mind for the elimination of evil, while Shinto looks to the outside world, and indeed does not concern itself with correcting evil or promoting good but merely with the acceptance of the existence of good and evil.

Buddhism now appears to take a higher profile in Japanese society than Shinto, partly because it is an internationally organised religion. It is also partly because there are Japanese sects within Buddhism, like the *Soka Gakkai*, which formed its own political party in 1964. This party, *Komeito*, or 'Clean Government Party', has played a significant role in Japanese politics since its foundation. Sects like *Soka Gakkai* and others claim millions of adherents, making it look as though virtually all Japanese have strong religious affiliations. However, most Japanese will say that they believe in a variety of religions, and they make use of the appropriate ritual at the appropriate time.

There are ancient and modern Buddhist temples throughout Japan, including some of the most famous monuments in the country. The Great Buddha of Kamakura, for example, was built in the thirteenth century, while the *Kinkaku-ji* and the *Ginkaku-ji*, the Golden Pavilion and the Silver Pavilion in Kyoto, were built in the fourteenth and fifteenth centuries and still attract thousands of visitors throughout the year.

Zen Buddhism

There are probably ten or more major Buddhist sects active in Japan, but Japan's great contribution to world Buddhism is Zen. Zen Buddhism originally came from China in the twelfth century, and its appeal to the Japanese warrior caste was immediate. Its influence on the way of the samurai *(Bushido)* was intense. Japanese monks and ascetics developed their own style of Zen, which has become peculiarly Japanese in its philosophy and appeal.

Followers of Zen seek enlightenment by meditation and the teaching of emptiness, a process that is achieved by, among other things, contemplating a series of unanswerable riddles. Each follower is expected to work out his way of salvation by means of physical and mental austerity and self-discipline, so that he can achieve the will power and inner strength demanded of the *samurai*.

CONFUCIANISM

The main moral underpinning of the Japanese way of life is not, however, Buddhism but another imported philosophy, Confucianism. Kong Fuzi (559 – 479 BC), whose name has been westernised as Confucius, was a comparatively minor Chinese government official who developed a code of behaviour based on both hierarchy and merit. Confucianism made its way to Japan probably as early as the fifth century AD, and has been at the heart of the structure of Japanese society ever since.

Confucianism promotes both the preservation of a rightful order, typified by his emphasis on filial piety (the obedience a son owes his father), and advancement by merit, as shown by his encouragement of scholarship and education. Confucianism as propagated during the years of the Tokugawa *shoguns* (say 1610 to 1860) was one that served not only to petrify the *status quo* into four unbreakable class divisions – with the *samurai* at the top, of course – but also kept women in a servile position.

A Japanese woman was throughout her life meant to be subservient to men, firstly to her father, secondly to her husband and finally to her son. 'Consider your husband as your master, respect him and serve him deferentially' was a typical injunction in the widely-read *Onna Daigaku* (*The Great Learning for Women*), which was published in the eighteenth century. The lot of women has changed a great deal since then, but Japan is still a man's country.

CHRISTIANITY

Christianity first came to Japan in the sixteenth century, but has never been accepted as anything other than a foreign religion.

Fewer than one percent of Japanese would claim to be practising Christians, although its image is greater than that in the main cities because you will see a few churches and, more noticeably, many young couples like to include a Christian element in their marriage ceremonies. The white bridal gown and veil are fashionable items for Japanese brides. Then there is Christmas, with the story of the infant Jesus, which is well known in Japan. There are all denominations of Christians in Japan, along with Mormons, Quakers and Jehovah's Witnesses, but it is still very rare and surprising to meet a Japanese who fully espouses the Christian faith.

JAPANESE MORAL CODES

As a general rule, and at the risk of over-simplifying a complicated subject, one could say that Japanese moral values are relative while western moral values are absolute. Most great western religions teach a set of rules which are eternal truths. The Ten Commandments teach us that 'thou shalt not kill', which means it is wrong to kill under any circumstances at any time. Of course, the West does not live up to the standards set by the Ten Commandments or the other moral teachings of Judaism, Christianity and Islam, but we are taught in absolutes of right and wrong.

Oriental philosophies, on the other hand, and Japanese moral codes in particular, teach how to behave in different circumstances. Certainly there is a law against murder in Japan, and as a general rule it is best to follow the philosophy of not killing one's neighbours. But everything is relative – there are circumstances in which it is better to kill than not to kill. Moral absolutes are intransigent and wrong to Japanese ways of thinking.

3

Japan Past

Japan's history defines its people and their actions today. As with any nation, there are certain key events in their history that still exert a significant effect on the national psyche.

THE JAPANESE PEOPLE

Early immigrants

The Japanese people are not as homogeneous as we might believe. The first inhabitants of what is now Japan would have moved across Asia to what was then the coastal limit of the Asian landmass probably around 50,000 to 80,000 years ago. The earliest unchallenged archaeological finds date back to around 50,000 years ago, and by the late Palaeolithic Period (say 15,000 years ago) there are a number of clear signs of human habitation. However, there were new influxes of immigrants from the south and from what was now becoming the Korean peninsula over the next several hundreds of years, and today's Japanese nation is a mixture of a variety of different peoples: Chinese, Korean, Ryukyuan and Ainu (the indigenous natives of the archipelago, now almost extinct, no more than a tourist attraction in northern Japan). One study concluded that there were so many different immigrations to the Japanese archipelago between about 700 BC and 500 AD that over 90% of the gene pool (of over one million people by that time) was of immigrant stock.

The first Japanese state

Although the official date of the beginning of the Emperor

Jimmu's reign is given as 660 BC, it is generally estimated that the first organised state in Japan, with a clear leader who can be described as an emperor, was established in the Yamato region of Japan, around modern Kyoto and Nara, in the second or third century AD.

By the fifth century AD, there is clear evidence of organised rule, and there is also evidence of trade and other contacts with the kingdom of Silla on the south-eastern tip of the Korean peninsula. Japan was a thriving and busy place, and the evidence of the massive tombs of their emperors, such as that of the fifth century Emperor Nintoku still dominating the landscape near Osaka, shows not only that their leaders were very powerful within their society, but also that they were able to organise vast numbers of men to labour on public projects.

The influence of Prince Shotoku

The first great hero of Japanese history is Prince Shotoku (*Shotoku Taishi*), the second son of Emperor Yumei, who became regent to his aunt, the Empress Suiko, in 594 AD. He was at the heart of the adoption of Buddhism into Japan, being the driving force behind the building of hundreds of temples. He was also very influential in the creation of the written Japanese language, the hybrid that grew out of Chinese characters. The reason that he is remembered to the extent that his image still features on banknotes, however, is that he instituted the *Taika* reforms of 604 AD, designed to strengthen the power of central government, and in the process created a nation which endures to this day.

He attempted to bring in Confucian ideals of advancement by merit, and created 12 ranks that were to be attained by courtiers according to their abilities rather than their birth. However, over the years the Japanese turned his ideals on their head and for hundreds of years court and government positions were handed on from generation to generation through the same family, the only merit involved being the merit of birth. The hierarchical structure of mediaeval and feudal Japan, from 600 to 1868, had its beginnings in Prince Shotoku's *Taika* reforms.

A civilised capital city

In 694 AD the first Chinese style city built on a grid layout was founded in the Asuka region south-east of present-day Osaka. This city only served as the capital for 16 years, before the government moved a short distance north, to a new and much grander city which they named *Heijo-kyo*, or Nara. For most of the eighth century, when Europe was still struggling through the war- and disease-stricken dark ages following the collapse of the Roman Empire, Japan's capital at Nara was a haven of advanced civilisation, and, inevitably, of political intrigue.

THE IMPERIAL LINE

Japan's imperial line has endured through 125 emperors and almost 2,000 years, but even as early as the Nara period, the true authority was passing out of the hands of the emperor and into those of his chief courtiers. The first family of the time was the Fujiwara family, and they quickly became adept at cementing their influence within the imperial household.

The rules of imperial succession had been settled by the Emperor Keitai in the early sixth century, rules which stipulated that the title should pass from generation to generation rather than from brother to brother (or sister to sister – women were not barred from inheriting the throne until the eighteenth century), but that did not stop people from trying to exert their own influence on the choice of emperor. What is more, throughout the first thousand years or so of the imperial line, it was common for the emperor or empress to abdicate in favour of the next generation and retire to a monastery, making the appointment of the regent a crucial one. Of the 125 emperors to date, over 60 – practically half of them – have abdicated rather than died on the throne.

The power of the Fujiwara clan

The way the Fujiwara clan secured their grip around the throat of the imperial family was simple. For several generations, the search for a suitable bride for the reigning emperor usually ended when they got to the Fujiwara home. There were always suitable daughters of the household available to be wed to the current emperor, and for years the empress was likely to be the daughter or the sister of the regent.

The natural next step after the marriage was the birth of a child, who was, of course, not only heir to the throne but also the grandson of the Fujiwara regent. As soon as the child was old enough to walk and talk, or at least as soon as it was clear he had survived the first difficult years of his life, the regent would put pressure on the emperor (his son-in-law) to abdicate and spend his declining years perhaps in a monastery surrounded by his friends and away from the responsibilities of being emperor. This pressure was usually too great for any but the very strongest emperors to fight against, and the result would be a young boy on the throne as emperor, with all the power wielded by his grandfather, acting of course entirely in his imperial grandson's name.

Power behind the throne

This process was repeated often enough through early Japanese history for it to be considered national policy. It has also become a national trait that can still be seen in Japanese society, and the Japanese business world, today. The man who wields the true power is not necessarily the man with the most powerful title. In Japan, rank and responsibility are often separate. Even today, the authority in a large corporation will not necessarily reside with the man with the most exalted title on his business card. There is always likely to be a power behind the throne.

The Fujiwara's tactics were so successful that they became the norm in politics as well. Throughout Japanese history, the role of the emperor has been sacred and inviolate, even if the dignity of the person holding that office has not been. The Fujiwara clan never tried to overthrow the emperor and usurp the throne for themselves; they merely made themselves indispensable to the imperial family, and as distributors of all the ranks and titles within the court, equally indispensable to all the lower ranked courtiers. Their title was inherited just as much as the title of emperor was and the loyalty expressed by the regents to the throne was handed down from generation to generation along with the authority and the trappings of power.

Plots against the Fujiwara family

It became inevitable that after several generations, the Fujiwara clan dominance would cause resentment among other families at court, and this in turn led to violence. The capital, which had moved from Nara to Kyoto (*Heian-kyo*, as it was originally known) in 794 AD, was regularly torn by factional strife as one family after another plotted against the Fujiwara. But for many years it was all to no avail. From the middle of the tenth century for another hundred years, there was a Fujiwara regent in power with an infant – or at best young adult – emperor on the throne. To add to the influence they wielded, it was the custom for a new husband to live in the bride's family home, so that the children of the union lived with their maternal grandparents. In the imperial case, this meant that young and future emperors were brought up in the regent's family home.

Tales of court life

We have a wonderful picture of eleventh century Japanese court life from the great Japanese book, often described as the world's first novel, *The Tale of Genji (Genji Monogatari)*, written by an obscure court lady about whom very little is known except her probable name – Murasaki Shikibu. It is a huge sweeping work of fiction, written in the early years of the eleventh century, based on Japanese court life, and is without doubt one of the great works of world literature. Murasaki also left us her diary as a further key to the life of a Japanese courtier a millennium ago, and her near contemporary Sei Shonagon wrote her brilliant and often very funny *Pillow Book* (*Makura no Soshi*) which documents the likes and dislikes of courtiers and the tedium and excitements of court life.

CENTURIES OF WAR

It became inevitable that the power of the Fujiwaras would not last for ever, but it was not until armed rebellion against their power sprang up that the change would prove to be possible. The weakness of the Fujiwara rule was that they did not have a standing army, and indeed based their entire social system on the fact that the country was at peace. This was true enough around

Kyoto and its environs, but in other parts of the country there was little peace, especially in the north where the indigenous Ainu people fought continuing guerrilla style battles against the encroaching Japanese. These areas were the training grounds for the warriors who would eventually prove to be the downfall of the Fujiwara. Two families in particular, the Taira clan and the Minamoto clan, became highly skilled warriors while the Fujiwara grew ever more effete.

Eventually, in a struggle that was more about the disgruntled state of ex-emperors in the priesthood and the frustrated ambitions of court outsiders than the failings of the Fujiwara regents, a civil war broke out, pitting them against the rebel clans. It is worth pointing out that in this civil strife, as in all internal conflicts in Japan up to the present day, all sides claimed to be fighting for the emperor. Nobody ever fought a battle in Japan to overthrow an emperor, although some had that effect.

THE RULE OF THE MINAMOTO CLAN

It was not until 1185, with the decisive naval battle of Dannoura, that these civil wars ended with the Minamoto clan in charge. They moved their capital to Kamakura, south of what is now Tokyo, and took for themselves the title *Shogun*, which like all good Japanese titles was then handed down through the generations. *Shogun* is the Japanese for 'general' or 'military leader' (in full, the rank was *Sei-I-Tai-Shogun*, which means 'Great Barbarian Conquering General').

The rule of the sword

From now on in Japan, the rule of the court, of gentility and civility, was replaced by the rule of the sword. The warriors had replaced the politicians. The emperors continued to reign in Kyoto, sustained (just about) by a court that had no authority and virtually no money, but which still maintained the inherent mystery and prestige of being led by the descendant of the Sun Goddess. All the business of running the country had moved to Kamakura.

The nobility of failure

At this stage it is worth mentioning one of the great heroes of Japanese history, Minamoto no Yoshitsune. Yoshitsune was the younger brother of Minamoto no Yoritomo, who was the ultimate victor after the Battle of Dannoura and went on to rule Japan as *Shogun* and establish a style of government that was to endure for another 700 years. Yoshitsune, on the other hand, was a tragic hero whose death in a hopeless cause marks him out forever as one of the great role models of Japan.

Popular myth has overtaken historical fact in the case of Yoshitsune, who is seen as a dashing, popular hero who could not be allowed to live because, by his very charm and popularity, he would always pose a threat to the rule of his brother – a cold, jealous and heartless power-hungry warrior. There is no need to go into the details of his career or of his final stand with his loyal retainer Benkei against the overwhelming odds of his brother's army, but there is no doubt that the image presented even today by popular films and books based on his life is no better than a half truth.

Yoshitsune was probably a man who could not settle for a peaceful life and always found a reason to be stirring up trouble that he would then have to quell. His brother, who seems to have the place in Japanese legend reserved for the Sheriff of Nottingham in the English equivalent, was probably no more nor less barbaric than his contemporaries, in an era remembered for its extreme ruthlessness. But the affection within the Japanese psyche for noble failures is personified in Yoshitsune. As the late Ivan Morris points out in his brilliant book, *The Nobility of Failure*, 'in battle he was imaginative and daring, in private life spontaneous, trusting and sincere. But above all he was loved for his misfortune and defeat... Yoshitsune's brilliant success during his fighting years was a prerequisite for his greatness, since it made the subsequent collapse all the more impressive and poignant.'

There is even, as Morris points out, a Japanese word, *hoganbiiki*, which literally means 'sympathy with the lieutenant' – Yoshitsune's rank in the Imperial Police – which denotes not merely sympathy for the underdog, which is a common enough emotion around the world, but sympathy with the losing side. That is a Japanese trait which still pervades its society today.

JAPAN MEETS THE WEST

In 1543, a ship was wrecked on the island of Tanegashima off the southern coast of Kyushu, causing three unfortunate Portuguese sailors to be able to claim the title of the first Westerners to reach Japan. This was an event that changed the course of the history of Japan, in many different ways. The Portuguese brought with them firearms and Christianity, both of which were to have a far-reaching effect on Japan over the next one hundred years.

The introduction of firearms

The arrival of the Westerners in Japan (the Portuguese were soon followed by the Spanish and the Dutch) coincided with a period of extreme civil strife in Japan, as the Shogunate set up almost four centuries earlier began to crumble. In the 1540s, there were several regional lords who were fighting for supremacy as the central authority of Japan fell apart. The arrival of a new and supreme weapon in the shape of the Portuguese arquebus meant that the Europeans were greeted with eagerness by the local warlords, and it did not take long for the new weapon to prove its superiority on the battlefield.

In 1549, just six years after the Portuguese arrived, one military leader, Oda Nobunaga (1534–1582), purchased 500 muskets for his troops. They were already being made in Japan by this time, and typically the Japanese craftsmen had made improvements to the European design so that they could now be used effectively in the rain and in the dark. This meant that the Japanese product was rather better than the imported version – a state of affairs that has prevailed ever since in Japanese manufacturing industry.

Muskets were used in several battles over the next few years. The authority of the central government had completely broken down, and rival feudal lords fought for control of the country, or at least their part of it. The battle that persuaded even the most traditional of Japanese warlords that the new western weapon was a necessity was the siege of Nagashino Castle on 29 June 1575, where Oda Nobunaga defended the castle against the assault of several thousand mounted *samurai*. His 3,000 musketeers slaughtered the heavily but traditionally armed *samurai* cavalry and secured a victory that was noted across the whole country. From then on, the use of firearms became a key skill for all fighting men in Japan.

A united Japan

Nobunaga, who was a cruel, duplicitous man, is nevertheless rightly regarded as one of the founders of modern Japan. His ambition, as stated on his personal seal, was 'to bring the whole country under one sword', a goal he only fell short of because he was assassinated before he could claim hegemony over the entire nation.

The credit for uniting all Japan must go to a small but immensely strong peasant who gave himself the name Toyotomi Hideyoshi. Toyotomi, the family name he adopted after using several other family names as he rose from obscurity to supreme power, means 'abundant provider', which is how he wished to be remembered. Hideyoshi was a menial retainer in Nobunaga's service who proved himself a great fighter, tactician and general. Within eight years of his mentor's death, he was undisputed controller of all Japan.

Heroes of mediaeval Japan

After he died, peacefully in 1598, his son failed to hold on to the reins of power. Within two years a decisive battle, at Sekigahara near Lake Biwa between present-day Nagoya and Kyoto, had effectively transferred power to the third great Japanese general of this era, Tokugawa Ieyasu (1542–1616). Ieyasu went on to found the dynasty of Tokugawa *shoguns* who transferred their headquarters to a small fishing village called Edo, and from there ruled Japan for the next two and a half centuries. They were three men of very different styles, but they are revered today as heroes of mediaeval Japan, and as leaders whose methods are still studied today.

Three styles of leadership

The story goes that Oda Nobunaga, Toyotomi Hideyoshi and Tokugawa Ieyasu were sitting together during one of their campaigns, watching a bird perched silently in a tree. Nobunaga, renowned for his cruelty and his threatening style, said, 'If that bird does not sing, I will kill it.' In today's management terms, his leadership style is seen as not persevering with somebody who cannot do the job – get rid of him and try somebody else.

Hideyoshi, a man of significant charm and powers of persuasion, said, 'If that bird does not sing, I will persuade it to sing.' The manager who uses persuasion – which may include extreme moral pressure – to get his men to work effectively, is seen as a Hideyoshi-type leader.

Ieyasu, the man who waited until the time was right to take control of the country, said, 'If that bird does not sing, I will wait until it does.' Birds sing: they do not need to be taught or persuaded. You just have to wait until the time is right.

These three different attitudes to making things happen are considered to embody the three different styles of management in Japan. But the preferred method is that of Ieyasu: wait and you will get what you want. Patience and persistence are cardinal virtues in Japan.

THE TOKUGAWA ERA

One of the first acts of the Tokugawa family as they set about consolidating their power was to banish all foreigners from Japan, and in particular to banish all traces of Christianity, a faith they considered subversive and a direct danger to the hard-won peace that had been re-established, rather forcibly, across the nation. The Tokugawa government wished to establish itself as the undisputed ruler of the country, and therefore took upon itself the control of various elements in Japanese society that until now had been considered beyond the powers of the court, or perhaps just beneath its dignity. So matters such as foreign affairs, the issuance of currency and the control of what people read, learned and thought became central to their system of rule. Christianity was the first philosophy to be proscribed.

The key to the longevity and the stagnation of the Tokugawa government, or *Bakufu* as it was known in Japanese, was its policy of isolation from the rest of the world.

Closed to outsiders

Once the Tokugawa clan and its allies had established their superiority, they set about making sure that nothing would ever overthrow it by excluding all foreigners from the country and banning the practice of the foreign religion, Christianity. Hideyoshi had already seen the dangers of this alien way of life, and issued edicts as early as 1587 restricting the practice of Christianity and banishing all missionaries, but it was not until the Tokugawa *Bakufu* took control that the exclusion policy took full effect.

In 1614, a decree expelled all missionaries and was followed up by mass crucifixions of Christians in Japan and of any foreign missionaries foolish to have ignored the decree. In 1639, Ieyasu's heirs passed laws to end all trade with Portugal and all contacts with the outside world. There was one small exception, a small Dutch trading post was allowed to operate from reclaimed land in Nagasaki Bay, a peninsula called Deshima on which a Dutch trading post survived, and occasionally thrived, for the next 200 years and more. But effectively Japan was closed to all outside influences.

A feudal hierarchy

This allowed the Tokugawa *shoguns* to strengthen their grip on Japan, and to establish their feudal hierarchy, divided into four classes which were unchangeable, in theory at least. At the top of the pile were the *samurai*, the warrior class who were the only class of people allowed to take part in government and the only people allowed to own property. Beneath them came the peasants who in theory at least were highly respected as the class that produced the food – especially the rice – that kept Japan going. Beneath the peasants came the artisans, the makers of all the clothes, utensils, tools and other implements that every *samurai* and every farmer needed. Finally, on the bottom rung came the merchants, the parasites who bought and sold things but, in the eyes of the *samurai*, were of no value to society.

These four classes were fixed: if you were born a peasant you would die a peasant and there could be no changes within the system. In practice, however, the *samurai*, who as a warrior class in peacetime had little to do except make mischief for themselves, soon found themselves heavily in debt to the merchant class, who were quite content to be at the bottom of the feudal pile if it also meant that they had money to spend. The feudal system endured because nobody dared to change it, because it suited Japan after centuries of war and because the Tokugawa *Bakufu* used a very thorough system of checks and spies to ensure that no rebellion was likely or even possible. It also survived because there was no outside stimulus for change.

A flowering of artistic life

The Tokugawa period was also an era of great flowering of
Japan's artistic life. Peace meant that great writers, painters,
playwrights and poets could not only have the time to create their
masterpieces but also there was a huge and rather idle public that
was eager to read, watch, listen and look at their works. Most of
the giants of Japanese arts were active during the seventeenth,
eighteenth and early nineteenth centuries – the playwright
Chikamatsu Monzaemon, the poet Basho, the artists Hokusai,
Hiroshige and Utamaro, among many others whose influence has
been felt on art all around the world.

The Way of the Warrior

It was also a time during which the philosophy of *Bushido* – the
Way of the Warrior – was refined and raised to a central place in
Japanese society. *Bushido* might have seemed singularly
inappropriate for the longest period of continued peace in
Japanese history, but because it emphasised self-denial, unthinking
obedience to one's lord and a great deal of ceremony, etiquette
and formal behaviour, it was espoused by the government as the
way the *samurai* should live. Of course, *samurai*, being human, did
not always live up to these lofty ideals. Sometimes they
deliberately did not do so.

The Forty-Seven *Ronin*

The greatest heroic tragedy of *samurai* times is the story of the
Forty-Seven *Ronin*, or masterless *samurai*. The *ronin* were
masterless because their lord, Asano, was forced to commit
suicide in 1700 after being provoked into insulting a senior
government official. The *ronin*, following the code of *Bushido*,
wished to avenge the death of their lord but knew they would be

closely watched by the government. They therefore scattered to avoid observation and lived lives of debauchery and petty crime to allay suspicion that they were planning any revenge. Almost three years later, on a suitably romantically snowy February night in 1703, they forced their way into their enemy's mansion and took his life. Patience and persistence achieved their ends again.

The Forty-Seven *Ronin* (who as noble failures were proud to commit ritual suicide after killing Lord Asano) are thought of as great heroes even today, because they represent virtues of loyalty, self-discipline and patience that are still highly valued. Japanese management style, for example, is one of continuous strategic thinking, of putting oneself into the position one would like to be in the future and working out how one would have got there, and the impact its achievement will have on all other aspects of the company's operation.

THE COMING OF THE BARBARIANS

The Tokugawa *shoguns* continued to govern Japan (while the emperor served little more than a ceremonial purpose at his court in Kyoto) until the middle of the nineteenth century. Japanese society had hardly progressed in those years, although the population grew so much that Kyoto, with a population in excess of 600,000 by 1700, was bigger than Paris. The economy was stagnant, as was the rest of society, but there was still no real internal pressure for change. Everyone had become used to the *status quo*.

Shipwrecked sailors

The Japanese certainly learned of the war that broke out between Britain and China in 1839, through the Dutch at Nagasaki, but this threat to China merely confirmed to them that isolation from the rest of the world was the best option. It was something that they could not possibly have catered for that finally began the process that brought Japan back into the community of nations – the United States began opening up the west coast of America. The process began in the 1830s and was accelerated by the discovery of gold in California in 1849. One of the effects of this greater population on the west coast of America was an increase in shipping across the North Pacific, especially between San Francisco and China. Some of these ships were shipwrecked on the coasts of Japan, and the sailors were, according to the laws of Japan, summarily executed.

Relations with America

In 1853, the Americans sent a mission to Japan, under the command of Commodore Matthew Perry, to insist that Japan treat foreign sailors fairly, and at the same time to attempt to open trading and diplomatic relations. The 'black ships', as they are known, sailed into what is now Tokyo Bay and Perry began negotiations with the Tokugawa officials. These talks were in danger of getting nowhere until Perry demonstrated his technological superiority by means of a little light bombardment of the shoreline. Thereupon the Japanese decided that negotiation was the sensible option, and the *Bakufu* eventually agreed to the presence of an American consul in Japan, and to limited trade relations.

The Meiji Restoration

This move was not supported by many of the ancient enemies of the Tokugawa clan, who felt that the barbarians should be expelled. This led to a brief but vigorous civil war, which, by

1868, caused the abdication of the last of the Tokugawa *shoguns*, the establishment of a parliamentary system and the restoration of the emperor to his position as head of state (which theoretically he always was). The emperor's capital was moved from Kyoto to the shogun's capital, Edo, which was renamed Tokyo (which means 'eastern capital'), and modernisation began in earnest. The Meiji Restoration of 1868, named for the Emperor Meiji (meaning 'enlightened government'), is the date from which modern Japanese history is reckoned.

The end of the Tokugawa era was achieved in the end remarkably peacefully. The final *shogun*, Tokugawa Keiki, lived to a ripe old age as a wealthy and respected but nonetheless private citizen, and the new leaders, under the banners of democracy, led Japan rapidly into the modern age.

Modernisation

It was a typically Japanese experience. The war cry of those who overthrew the Tokugawas was '*Sonno Joi*', which roughly means, 'Revere the Emperor and expel the barbarians.' They certainly revered the emperor, but to achieve the overthrow of the *shoguns*, they had to make use of western fighting technology just as the first Tokugawa had done 250 years earlier. This time, however, the barbarians could not be expelled again.

We still see this curious mixture of clear vision mixed with extreme pragmatism in Japan today. The Japanese have a predilection for plans and strategies, which they stick to even when things go wrong, for far longer than Europeans or Americans would do. Quite often, the plan proves its worth after all, long after other cultures might have given up on it. But once the Japanese realise that a plan is hopeless, as for example the idea of expelling the barbarians after the 1860s, they change course dramatically. So eagerly did the Japanese embrace western ideas and methods that within 30 years of the fall of the feudal system, they had a government and an army which brought Japan into the first rank of nations. It was an astonishing achievement.

Learning from the West

The modernisation of Japan was no accident. The new government, having abolished the feudal class system and banned the wearing of swords in public, set about learning from the West in a thoroughly efficient way. Official missions were sent around the world to discover the best that the West had to offer and bring it back to Japan. Thus, their naval technology was acquired from Britain, their army was trained by Germans and their bureaucracy was based on French methods. They learned about western education, western production techniques and western communications systems and brought the best back to Japan.

It was an astonishing leap forward by a backward nation, but a nation that was used to being ordered, peaceful and hardworking. The plans were laid down and then carried out. It was probably the greatest example of sustained national effort for peaceful purposes that has been witnessed in modern times. It did not take long for the West to understand that Japan was a power to be reckoned with.

THE ROAD TO WAR

The one trouble with all this progress (looking back with the benefit of hindsight and the moral attitudes of the twenty-first century) was that the countries Japan had modelled herself on –

Britain, France, Germany, the United States – were all nations that had achieved their exalted position by military might. Japan learnt, without having to be taught, that might is right. If they meant to rank with the great nations of the world, then they also had to be a fearsome opponent.

The Russo-Japanese War

When this example from outside was coupled with the *Bushido* code so devoutly espoused by many of the anti-Tokugawa faction who were now part of the Meiji government, the result was a constitution that placed the military at the very centre of government. The first attempts by the new Japan to go to war were satisfyingly successful. The Russo-Japanese War of 1904/05, which was fought largely for dominance in the Korean peninsula and in Manchuria, was a bloody affair in which the Japanese lost tens of thousands of lives.

It finished in a naval battle in the straits of Tsushima, between Japan and Korea, in which Admiral Togo's fleet (built in Britain) took on the Russian fleet that had sailed all the way from the Baltic, round the Cape of Good Hope and up towards their home base of Vladivostok. The Russians were exhausted and ill-prepared even before the Japanese navy (which had sailed no more than a couple of hundred nautical miles) tore into them. It was a slaughter, with the Russian fleet losing 34 ships and almost 5,000 men in little more than 12 hours of engagement.

The battle was Japan's, the war was over and Japan secured the rights it had sought in Korea. Warfare works: that was the message Admiral Togo brought home.

Lack of acceptance from the West

Throughout the first three decades of the twentieth century, Japan matched the western nations in its aspirations for international respect through military might, but it was an impossible task for Japan to be accepted as an equal by the western powers. After the First World War, in which Japan invoked its obligations to Britain under the Anglo-Japanese Alliance of 1902, western acknowledgement of its Asian ally was muted. Japan's proposal for a racial equality clause to be inserted in the covenant of the League of Nations was rejected, and their government also had to accept a smaller size of navy than Britain and the United States. Despite the huge achievements of the previous 50 years, and Japan's unwavering support for the British and American causes, any sense of an equal footing alongside the leading nations of the world was denied to Japan.

Influence of the military

Japan's western-influenced constitution demanded that no cabinet could be complete without a minister of war, and that this minister had to be a serving officer in one of the armed services. In the early years of Japan's post-restoration development, this was not a particularly important point, but as political dissatisfaction and economic unrest after the First World War began to grip Japan, the services realised that by refusing to appoint a war minister to any cabinet they disapproved of, they had a controlling influence on the politics of Japan.

The Great Kanto Earthquake of 1 September 1923, which destroyed much of Tokyo and Yokohama and left over 100,000 people dead, added to the chaos that was beginning to spread across Japan, and the army, in particular, realised that it was time they interceded in Japanese political life.

The Second World War

It was the influence of the military on the civilian government that ultimately led Japan on the path to war, coupled with the national sense of injustice in the attitude of western governments to peoples that they clearly considered inferior. During the 1930s, Japan carved out an empire – the 'Greater East Asia Co-Prosperity Sphere' was the Orwellian English translation – and in 1941 attacked the United States at Pearl Harbor.

Understanding the behaviour of the Japanese soldiers

The actions of the Japanese soldiers during the war years cannot be condoned or defended, but it is worth looking from a different viewpoint to gain some understanding of how they came about. The Japanese army were trained to obey every order without question, to fight to the death and to consider surrender a fate worse than death. People who surrendered before their onslaughts, rather than fight to the death, were already shamed in the eyes of the Japanese, and had forfeited any hope of respect or sympathy. So prisoners were treated as though their lives were already over, which to their Japanese captors they were. The Geneva Convention did not enter their thoughts: the reasoning that went into creating that document was entirely alien to the Japanese.

The Japanese have also always distinguished between behaviour where you are known and behaviour where you are not known, a variation on our old friends *uchi* and *soto*. The Japanese soldiers were not at home, bound by the rules of their own society, and so those rules did not apply. It is a weak excuse in western terms but even today we see instances of appalling behaviour by Japanese abroad (a weekend sex orgy for 300 Japanese businessmen and 400 Chinese prostitutes in a hotel in China is a recent example).

The shame of the journey, as the Japanese saying goes, is forgotten at home.

THE AFTERMATH OF WAR

The Second World War ended in August 1945, with the dropping of two atomic bombs, one on Hiroshima and one on Nagasaki. Without arguing the morality of using nuclear weapons, the Americans clearly believed that their deployment would shorten the war and thereby save lives. The effect on the Japanese, not surprisingly, has been deep and long lasting. As the only nation ever to have suffered a nuclear attack, they feel very strongly that the use of such weapons is wrong, and every year the memorial events in Hiroshima and Nagasaki serve to remind the Japanese of their special position in the nuclear debate.

It is a subject that an outsider ventures into with extreme care: I have yet to meet a Japanese who feels that the use of atomic bombs was justified and any frivolous discussion about the events of August 1945 can cause great offence. Oddly, the Japanese rarely focus on why the Americans felt the need to drop the bombs, but this is in part because the history books used in Japanese schools skim fairly lightly over the latter part of the Second World War. Many Japanese just do not know, because they have never been told, the full story of their fathers' and grandfathers' activities in the 1930s and 1940s.

A new strategy

For the Japanese, and for the rest of the world, the atom bombs were a turning point in their history. The policies of the first half of the century had failed, so a completely new strategy had to be devised and followed. The Americans, once the hated enemy, now became Japan's closest friends. The new constitution, put together by the Americans on behalf of the defeated Japanese, renounced war for all time and prohibited Japan from ever maintaining armed forces. Winning the respect of the rest of the world by military means had failed, so from now on the effort would be made to succeed by economic means.

The history of the past 50 years is the story of Japanese industry, management and business practices which have been far more effective in securing a prosperous lifestyle for the Japanese than any military adventures could possibly have been.

4

The Cultural Values of Japan

During the 1970s, one of the European Union's commissioners was involved in negotiations with the Japanese over a particularly difficult trade issue. The talks were not going well, and in a confidential briefing to commercial staff at several European embassies in Tokyo, the commissioner admitted that he found it impossible to deal with the Japanese. 'They are from another planet,' he was quoted as saying. 'They are not Earthmen.'

AN 'ALIEN' CULTURE

The Japanese are Earthmen, and in the vast majority of their actions and reactions, they are similar to all other Earthmen. As Shakespeare noted about another race that has been consistently misunderstood, if you prick them, do they not bleed? If you tickle them, do they not laugh? Indeed, it may well be that the Japanese are easier to deal with than people from cultures nearer to our own. At least with the Japanese you know you are dealing with an alien culture – they look different, they speak a different language and they eat different food for a start – so the visitor is much more likely to be aware of misunderstandings than a British visitor to Germany, for example. At least when misunderstandings are noticed, there is a chance of correcting them.

WA – THE HARMONY OF EXISTENCE

Many different analysts, both from within and outside Japan, have tried to identify what it is that makes the Japanese different from other Earthmen. Some of their conclusions agree with each other, and some do not. Most people would agree, though, that at the heart of Japanese society is the continuous search for *wa*. *Wa* is a virtually indefinable term, usually translated as 'harmony'. It has overtones of peacefulness and fulfilment within its meaning, and is the essence of how Japanese life should be lived.

The sound 'wa' also means 'peace' and is an ancient name for Japan itself. If we begin with the idea that everything a Japanese does, thinks or touches has a rightful place in the world, and that this place should not be upset by thoughts or actions that upset the harmony of existence, then we have the starting point for explaining the logic (but 'logic' is a western term, of course) behind the actions of the Japanese.

In 1937, the Japanese Ministry of Education issued a document entitled 'Fundamentals of our National Polity' *(Kokutai no Hongi)*, and while much of what is in that document has inevitably been superseded by history, the paragraphs on the meaning of harmony remain true today. 'Harmony as in our nation is a great harmony of individuals who, by giving play to their individual differences, and through difficulties, toil and labour, converge as one. Because of individual differences and difficulties, this harmony becomes all the greater and its substance rich.'

This may be an idealised view of how Japanese harmony works, but it is an ideal that the Japanese believe in. Japan, like many other East Asian cultures, works on a group ethic, but they take this principle to a different level. It is not simply that the good of the group must take precedence over the good of the individual;

the Japanese feel that the individual has a responsibility to develop personal skills (and to minimise personal defects) which are then used exclusively for the good of the group. Everybody is an individual, but every individual has his or her own unique and important place within a group.

A KIND OF EQUALITY

The Japanese would also say that this harmony produces an equality that is not found in other cultures. Japanese society, in certain obvious ways, is an equal, if not necessarily democratic, society. As Kenichi Ohmae put it in his ground-breaking book, *The Mind Of The Strategist*, 'grossly oversimplifying, one could say that in Japan, every member of the village is equal and a generalist.' The unique place that everybody has in the group, or village, or company, is equal to everybody else's place and is also interchangeable. While it is important that everybody has a particular skill that they bring to the group, such as the ability to build houses or do the accounts or cook *katsudon*, everybody is replaceable and interchangeable. The most important skill that anybody can bring to the group is the ability to be adaptable, and to perform successfully the tasks the group wants you to perform.

EQUALITY VERSUS FREEDOM

Equality and freedom are not often good bedfellows. The French Revolution, which espoused the three causes of liberty, equality and fraternity, soon found itself sacrificing liberty in the name of equality. A very free society, such as in the United States, is not particularly equal, and the Japanese trick of combining equality with liberty seems to go against the natural order of things, However, it is not really so. The freedom that Japanese people have in their lives, which they would all say is very real, is very much circumscribed by the needs of the group. True freedom of action, in the individual sense we understand in the West, is a rarity in Japan. The needs of the group must come first.

This striving for harmony has been noted by many observers of the Japanese and other cultures. The Japanese have a tendency to prove their culture is unique by comparing it with western cultures, as if to try and create a harmonious place for all cultures of the world. Western cultures are happy to stand on their own merits, without having to be compared as better or worse than others. Once again, we see the difference between the analogue and digital approaches to life.

WHAT WESTERNERS HAVE MADE OF JAPANESE CULTURE

A juvenile culture?

Perhaps the most famous of all comments about the Japanese was made by General Douglas MacArthur shortly after he took over as Supreme Commander of the Allied Powers in Japan in 1945. He called them 'a nation of twelve year olds'. What he meant by this comment was that to his American eyes, the Japanese were very keen and enthusiastic, very eager to help and very willing to learn. They were also very unsophisticated and very unable to foresee the consequences of their actions. Viewed from a western standpoint, his observation still has echoes today, but to describe the Japanese as unsophisticated, for example, would be a mistake.

Japanese women may sometimes appear to be annoyingly babyish and 'cute' to western eyes, giggling bashfully at every opportunity in public and decorating their apartments with teddy bears, but this is not childishness *per se*. It is simply a defence mechanism against the realities of a very masculine society.

The general Japanese preference for facts rather than opinions may appear to Westerners as juvenile, but that stems from their education system, where the accumulation of facts is rewarded and the expression of opinions, especially one's own opinions, is not encouraged. One foreign theatre producer, who had licensed a play to be performed in Japanese, came over to Tokyo for the opening night. The next morning he asked what the reviews in the newspapers had been like. 'We don't do reviews,' was the reply. 'We just record the facts, such as "There was a standing ovation".'

Change and authority

The first post-war book to try to analyse the culture of Japan was *The Chrysanthemum And The Sword* (1946), by the American anthropologist Ruth Benedict. Perhaps the two key characteristics of the Japanese that she identified in her truly brilliant thesis were the contradictory facts that the Japanese can change their society without challenging its underlying values, and that Japan 'is a triangle controlled by a pin in one corner'.

A triangle lying on a snooker table, for example, is easily visible, but the way it can be turned, and the side or corner on which it can be made to pivot, is unknown. In the same way, Japanese society is easy to see, but what controls its changes is harder to guess. Will it swivel on the top corner, or to the left or to the right? The architecture of the triangle has a top and a bottom, just as the hierarchy of society does. But the power in that hierarchy may well not be at the top. In fact, in Japanese society and in Japanese business, 'every effort is made to minimize the appearance of arbitrary authority, and to make every act appear to be a gesture of loyalty to the status-symbol who is so constantly divorced from real exercise of power'.

This is why Japanese ideas of leadership are so different from western concepts. Where in the West we look for certain qualities in our leaders – decisiveness, vision and man management skills perhaps, but above all visibility – in Japan the blatant exercise of authority is seen as somehow breaking the harmony of the group.

It is also explains why every warrior on every side in every civil war in Japan has always declared his loyalty to the emperor before going out to fight. In this way, Japanese can revolt against the *status quo* without becoming revolutionary. The civil war of the 1860s culminated in drastic change – the overthrow of the Tokugawa *shoguns* and the installation of parliamentary government. But this drastic change was called the Meiji Restoration, not the Meiji Revolution. Japan does not have breaks with the past, but at the same time she is eager to embrace the future.

Obligations and decision-making

In 1957, the then British Ambassador to Japan, Sir Esler Dening, retired. In his final letter to the Foreign Secretary he summed up his thoughts on the Japanese a decade after the end of the war. 'Material progress has been spectacular and industrially Japan today still ranks first in Asia. But the western ways and western ideas, apart from material progress, have by no means been assimilated.' Dening, who had been involved with Japan for almost 40 years, loved the country and the people but was not afraid to express his thoughts about them.

This contrasted, in his view, with the Japanese themselves. 'To ask a Japanese what he thinks is usually to be sure that he will not tell you... It has been said that almost from birth the Japanese are under such a load of obligations that they are never free to follow an independent course. It is for this reason that it is impossible to get an immediate decision from an individual; he must always consult first with all the people to whom he has obligations in the matter.' Nothing much has changed since then. Decisiveness is still a sin in Japan.

ANALYSING JAPANESE CULTURE

A recent social anthropologist who has studied the differences between cultures and come up with some interesting ideas about Japan is the Dutch professor Geert Hofstede. In his major work, *Cultures and Organisations*, he identifies the cultural pillars of over 50 national cultures, Japan included, and points out the similarities and differences that affect the way cultures relate to each other. He notes that there are five different dimensions to culture, and the way that cultures vary across these five dimensions pinpoints the different ways that cultures approach communication and problem-solving, which is, in most anthropologists' opinion, the point of a culture in the first place.

He identifies Japan as a collectivist culture. This does not come as a great surprise to anybody who has tried to deal with the Japanese, especially from the background of the three most individual national cultures: the United States, Australia and Britain. Japan is actually, according to Hofstede's research, reasonably middle-ranked on the world list of individualistic cultures, and there is no doubt that while most cultures have become slightly more collectivist over the past 30 years or so,

FARNHAM CASTLE
INTERNATIONAL BRIEFING &
CONFERENCE CENTRE

Hofstede's Cultural Parameters

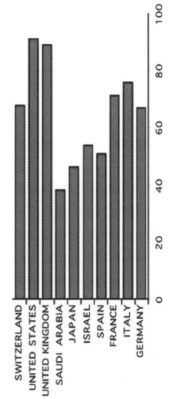

INDIVIDUALISM

Individualism:

'The extent to which individual interests prevail over collective interests.'

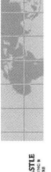

Hofstede's Cultural Parameters

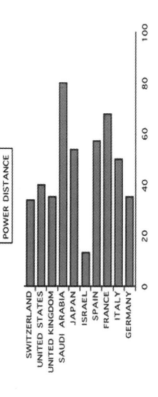

POWER DISTANCE

SWITZERLAND
UNITED STATES
UNITED KINGDOM
SAUDI ARABIA
JAPAN
ISRAEL
SPAIN
FRANCE
ITALY
GERMANY

0   20   40   60   80   100

Power distance:

'The extent to which less powerful members of institutions and organisations within a country accept and expect that power is distributed unequally.'

Japan has become more individualistic. Yet he uses Japanese examples of a collectivist society when he notes that 'the maintenance of harmony with one's social environment becomes a key virtue' in collectivist societies.

Dealing with inequality

Hofstede also identifies what he calls 'Power Distance' as a dimension of culture. Power Distance is basically the way that societies deal with inequality. All societies are unequal, but what Hofstede was looking for was the way that societies dealt with that inequality. The most hierarchical cultures, i.e. those most at ease with inequality, are generally those in which religion, whether Muslim or Roman Catholic, plays a central role. Malaysia, Arab cultures and South American countries head the list, while white egalitarian Europe scores the low scores. Israel is the one culture with a religious centre which scores very low on Power Distance, but Japan, which has a very hierarchical but comparatively unreligious past tradition, earns a very average score. As Hofstede suggests, the Japanese 'accept and appreciate inequality, but feel that the use of power should be moderated by a sense of obligation'. We are back with the understated notions of leadership that Ruth Benedict noted in the Japanese.

Masculinity and femininity

The third cultural dimension is that of masculinity or femininity. According to Hofstede, Japan is the most masculine society in the world, easily outranking the second most masculine, Austria. Masculinity is not simply a statement of whether men rule the roost, but whether 'masculine' values of possessions, competition and challenge are embraced rather than the 'feminine' values of co-operation and relationship building.

FARNHAM CASTLE
INTERNATIONAL BRIEFING &
CONFERENCE CENTRE

Hofstede's Cultural Parameters

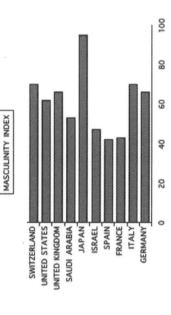

MASCULINITY INDEX

SWITZERLAND
UNITED STATES
UNITED KINGDOM
SAUDI ARABIA
JAPAN
ISRAEL
SPAIN
FRANCE
ITALY
GERMANY

0   20   40   60   80   100

Masculinity index:

'The extent to which people adopt masculine values of success, ambition and possessions rather than the feminine values of caring, compromise and quality of life.'

At first glance, it would appear that Japan should not score particularly highly on the masculine/feminine scale, because as we have seen, harmony, co-operation and relationship building are central to Japan's way of going about things. There is also the 'feminine' issue of lifetime job security, which was certainly the norm in Japan at the time that Hofstede was first carrying out his research, even if that has changed a little now. However, there are other issues, such as the incredibly high level of pressure and competition in Japan's education system, the lack of female managers in most areas of business and the concepts of inner strength as espoused by Zen Buddhism, which point towards a society with masculine values.

A study in 1986 (on the face of it one of the more unlikely studies to have received university funding) showed that three-month-old baby boys in Japan were significantly noisier than three-month-old baby girls, while the opposite was true in the United States. The study concludes that this difference was not likely to be inborn, but induced by the mother's expectations in each society. It also noted that adult Japanese males are noisier than adult Japanese females, while adult females are the noisy ones in any group of Americans. Japan is certainly still a man's world, even though it may gradually be changing.

Responding to uncertainty

Hofstede's fourth cultural dimension is something he calls 'Uncertainty Avoidance'. Uncertainty exists in life, but the way we deal with it helps define a group or culture. Uncertainty Avoidance is 'the extent to which the members of a culture feel threatened by uncertain or unknown situations'. On this parameter, Japan scores very high, while the British, Americans

FARNHAM CASTLE
INTERNATIONAL BRIEFING &
CONFERENCE CENTRE

Hofstede's Cultural Parameters

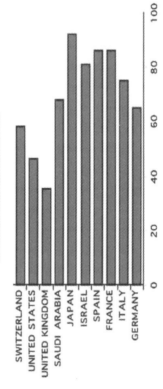

UNCERTAINTY AVOIDANCE

SWITZERLAND
UNITED STATES
UNITED KINGDOM
SAUDI ARABIA
JAPAN
ISRAEL
SPAIN
FRANCE
ITALY
GERMANY

0   20   40   60   80   100

Uncertainty avoidance:

'The extent to which members of a culture feel threatened by uncertain or unknown situations.'

and many Europeans score quite low. The Japanese in general are a far more anxious people than the British or Americans.

As Hofstede notes, 'In countries with strong uncertainty avoidance, people come across as busy, fidgety, emotional, aggressive and active.' Clearly, Japanese people do not seem to Westerners to be emotional or fidgety (compare a class of 15-year-old schoolchildren in Britain and Japan for degrees of fidgetiness) but the Japanese have been taught by convention to hide their emotions. Watch a Japanese businessman when he is released from his social obligations with the help of a few glasses of beer or whisky: then you will see emotion.

Precision and punctuality, two other attributes of those cultures who are unhappy with uncertainty, are other features of Japanese culture. In business terms, the Japanese fondness for facts and forward planning is another sign of their need to minimise uncertainty in their lives. Every company in the world produces a forward plan, but only in Japan will companies produce plans for 20 years hence.

The pyramid versus the village network
When Hofstede put together his results for Power Distance and Uncertainty Avoidance, he realised that national cultures fall broadly into four quadrants, according to whether they have weak or strong Power Distance coupled with weak or strong Uncertainty Avoidance. Japan, with figures on the high side for both categories, comes in the largest group of countries which he describes as having a 'pyramid of people' – in business terms with the general manager at the top of the pyramid and everybody in their proper place below.

Britain, the USA, Australia, Ireland and the Scandinavian countries, on the other hand, have comparatively low scores in each category, and therefore place themselves in the opposite quadrant. This means they follow what another scholar, the American Owen Stevens, calls the rules of the 'village market', which has little hierarchy or rules, but pragmatically follows the demands of the situation. These two business styles are far apart, and a culture that is based in the village market – practical, opportunistic and decisive – will find it very hard to work easily with those well ordered, regular and hierarchical types who prefer the pyramid of people.

Virtue versus truth

Hofstede's final cultural dimension is that of 'Long Term Orientation', which is not simply a case of forward planning, but what he calls the conflict between virtue and truth, between Confucian principles of virtue and western scientific ideals of truth. As one may guess, the Japanese and Chinese are at one end of this scale, with most Europeans and the Americans at the other end.

A survey was carried out by a Japanese consultancy firm, in which they asked people to name their 'favourite words' from a list of values. These 'favourite words' were not chosen for their sound but for the relevance of the values they indicated to the respondents' lives. The survey showed that the 'favourite words' of the Japanese were 'effort', 'perseverance' and 'thank you', while those of Europeans (a widely varying cultural group, of course) were 'family', 'love' and 'fun'. 'Effort' and 'perseverance' are two typically long-term values, while 'fun' in particular is of the moment. Neither set of values can be described as better than the other, but they are certainly different.

Hofstede's Cultural Parameters

LONG-TERM ORIENTATION

SWITZERLAND					
UNITED STATES					
UNITED KINGDOM					
SAUDI ARABIA					
JAPAN					
ISRAEL					
ITALY					
GERMANY					
FRANCE					

0   20   40   60   80   100

Long-term orientation:

'The extent to which a society can live without quick results and instant gratification.'

LEADERSHIP AND THE ORGANISATION

Other scholars have expanded on Hofstede's work, notably the Anglo-Dutch pair Charles Hampden Turner and Fons Trompenaars, who have shown how the national cultural characteristics apply to organisational culture, and how different cultures view concepts such as 'leadership' and 'corporate vision'. In particular, they measured the response in different cultures to the statement: 'A company is a system designed to perform functions and tasks in an efficient way. People are hired to perform these functions with the help of machines and other equipment. They are paid for the tasks they perform'.

Ninety per cent of Americans agreed with that statement, as did over 80% of British respondents. However, only about 25% of Japanese went along with the idea. They much preferred the statement: 'A company is a group of people working together. They have social relations with other people and with the organization. The functioning is dependent on these relations'.

In the one case, a company's task is to produce results, first and foremost for the shareholders, while in the other view, a company is an extension of society and functions only through the communal will of those within it. The two attitudes are fundamentally different. Partnerships between people or organisations basing their working methods on these almost mutually exclusive ideals will struggle to succeed.

A second statement that was put to different nationalities was: 'It is important for a manager to have at hand precise answers to most of the questions that his/her subordinates may raise about

FARNHAM CASTLE
INTERNATIONAL BRIEFING &
CONFERENCE CENTRE

The West is Task and Function Orientated

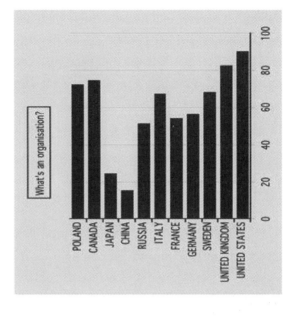

What's an organisation?

POLAND · CANADA · JAPAN · CHINA · RUSSIA · ITALY · FRANCE · GERMANY · SWEDEN · UNITED KINGDOM · UNITED STATES

(scale: 0, 20, 40, 60, 80, 100)

Percentage of people agreeing with the statement:

'A company is a system designed to perform functions and tasks in an efficient way. People are hired to perform these functions with the help of machines and other equipment. They are paid for the tasks they perform.'

Other respondents agreed with the statement:

'A company is a group of people working together. They have social relations with other people and with the organisation. The functioning is dependent on these relations.'

© Trompenaars Hampden-Turner Culture for Business

their work'. The concept that the boss should know how to direct his staff is one that provokes very different responses in different cultures. In Northern Europe and America, fewer than one quarter of all respondents agreed with that idea: for them the manager was not meant to know everything, and debate about questions raised at work is seen as normal and healthy.

The percentages agreeing with the statement get greater across southern Europe, but by the time we reach Japan, the figures show over three-quarters of business people agreeing with the concept. In Japan, you do not question the boss. Reconciling these two methods of running a company or a department or team across cultural divides is no mean achievement. However, being able to identify the issue is a good starting point.

HARMONY IN THE WORKPLACE

Harmony is, as we have seen, a key element in Japan's ability to exist with itself. The maintenance of harmony is more important than abstract concepts of truth and right. This leads, as we will see in the next chapter, to a great deal of deliberate ambiguity. Ambiguity is 'a weapon which enables one to co-exist harmoniously with others and to enjoy the benefits of insider status', according to the Japanese commentator Hiroshi Kagawa. 'Ambiguity avoids or smooths over conflicts and promotes teamwork, allowing one modestly to blend into the group'. This statement presupposes a common definition of 'teamwork', which is probably wishful thinking, but the maintenance of harmony is the overriding rule of the Japanese workplace. Conflict – on a personal level or within the team – is taboo.

The Boss Should Know

FARNHAM CASTLE
INTERNATIONAL BRIEFING &
CONFERENCE CENTRE

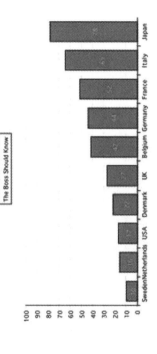

The Boss Should Know

Percentage agreeing with the statement: 'It is important for a manager to have at hand precise answers to most of the questions that his/her subordinates may raise about their work.'

High context and low context cultures

The American social scientist E T Hall has classified cultures in terms of 'low context' or 'high context'. A low context culture communicates through the words, while a high context culture will deliver the message as much through the person who delivers it as through the words it uses. In a high context culture key points are understood intuitively, action is built around relationships rather than tasks and they emphasise reaching agreement rather than completing a task. From these clues, it is easy to see that Japan is a high context culture, while much of Europe and America is much lower context.

The concept of high and low context works equally well with organisations. Some, like schools with their own language and rules, are comparatively high context: it takes outsiders some time to feel at home there. Others, like petrol stations for example, are very low context. They are there to fulfil a task – that of selling fuel, and maybe offering a car wash – but there is no sense of belonging or even of distinction between one petrol station and another.

When somebody joins an organisation, they inevitably have to join as a 'low context' person. Everything has to be explained to them clearly until they become familiar and understand certain things more intuitively. Japanese firms routinely run two or three week induction courses to give new recruits a real sense of the values of the organisation, while western managers just spend a couple of hours pointing out the fire exits and the coffee machine. Values and corporate missions in western firms are written in framed documents and hung on the walls of reception areas. In Japanese firms they are built into the way everybody goes about their work. Things are not spelled out.

It was the former British Labour chancellor Denis Healey who
quoted in his autobiography the startling statistic that 'Japan has
1,000 engineers for every hundred lawyers; the United States has
1,000 lawyers for every hundred engineers'. This is a typical
example not only of the inflated figures beloved by finance
ministers around the world (America has over 20 times as many
lawyers per capita as Japan, but not quite the overwhelming
difference that Healey implies) but also of the difference between a
high context culture that does things intuitively, and the low
context culture that has to have everything written down and
agreed before getting under way.

Lawyers do not breed harmony: they thrive on confrontation.
Japan just does not see the point of them.

5

The Japanese Language

It is said that the Japanese language is one of the two or three most difficult languages for native English speakers to learn. It is up there with Hungarian and Finnish at the top of the incomprehensibility charts. It is therefore beyond the scope of this book to give more than a basic smattering of Japanese words which might be of use to the visiting business person. If you want to learn the language, there is only one way to do it and that is through a concentrated learning programme and, even more importantly, constant practice in everyday life.

THE THINKING BEHIND THE WORDS

What we can look at within the context of this book is a basic understanding of the way that the language works, and the way it differs from the English language. Misunderstandings between people of different cultural and linguistic backgrounds do not usually originate in the words used to get the message across – they arise in the thinking behind the words and in the way the same words are used in different ways in different languages.

It is always wise to remember that almost every Japanese person, apart from a handful of virtually bilingual people, will be thinking in Japanese when they speak in English. This means that unless you understand the basic concepts of the way the Japanese language works, and the way thoughts and sentences are formed, you will run a very great risk of misunderstanding what they actually mean, as opposed to the words they speak. What is more, the same will be true for you speaking in English to all but the very best English speakers: your listeners will, to some extent at least, be translating your words back into Japanese, and drawing Japanese conclusions from the English words you have spoken. To make matters worse, more often than not, neither party will be aware that there has been any misunderstanding at all.

THE ORIGINS OF JAPANESE

Japanese and English are as different as two languages can be. Japanese is, in fact, different from every other language on the planet, bearing only very slight connections to any other language. There continues to be a scholarly debate on where the language originated, with experts noting connections with Korean, Finnish, Turkish and some Indian and Australasian languages, while other experts note no such connections and consider Japanese to be a hybrid of many other languages. Certainly, modern Japanese vocabulary borrows from Chinese and, inevitably, English, but the grammar, pronunciation and syntax is all its own.

READING AND WRITING JAPANESE

Perhaps the key issue in understanding Japanese is to look at the way it is written. It was very bad luck for the Japanese that their language developed first of all in a purely spoken form, and it was not until the first Buddhist missionaries came over from the mainland to Japan around the fifth century AD that the Japanese saw language written down. The bad luck for the Japanese was that the ideographic style of writing Chinese, where each character has a meaning but no phonetic element, was totally unsuited to writing Japanese. If Japan had been next door to Italy or Arabia, Greece or Russia, or almost anywhere rather than China, the Japanese language would have developed in a quite different way, and the learning of the language would not be the huge undertaking it is, for both foreigners and the Japanese themselves.

Japanese and Chinese – two very different languages

Chinese and Japanese could not be more different languages. Chinese is a language without verb endings, plurals, tense differentials or even, originally, more than one syllable to each word. What's more, it is spoken in a range of different tones, the meaning changing according to the tone used. Japanese, on the other hand, is a highly inflected language; with different verb endings for past, present and future; with different suffixes for subject and object; very polysyllabic; and without any tonal aspect.

In Chinese, a sentence is constructed with the subject of the sentence first, then the verb, then the object. In Japanese, the order is subject (if it is stated, which it often is not), object, verb. So, where the Chinese say, 'The man buys a book', the Japanese say, 'The man a book buys'. On top of this, Japanese is full of different levels of vocabulary according to whether the speaker is considered more or less important than the person they are talking to, whether the speaker is male or female and whether they are speaking highly informally, within the family for example. The vocabulary of the two languages was, originally, totally different, and the initial attempts by the Japanese to write their language using the Chinese script were an ignominious failure.

A Chinese character, for example, 日 has a clear meaning (sun), but the pronunciation of that character is not necessarily linked to its shape. This is a huge advantage in China, where the pronunciation of the language changes drastically across the country. Spoken Mandarin, the language of Beijing, is not readily understandable by Shanghainese, nor by Southern Chinese who speak Cantonese. But the written language is understandable by all. In Japan, where everybody speaks the same language, this absence of a phonetic link in the writing is a huge disadvantage.

The development of writing in Japanese

This presented a dilemma to the Japanese of 1,500 years ago when they first came across the idea of writing things down. They realised the advantages of not having to remember everything in their heads from now on, but they also recognised how difficult it would be to write Japanese using Chinese characters. There were basically three options. Firstly, they could carry on as before, as though the Chinese missionaries had never arrived, and continue with Japanese as purely a spoken language, used by a people who had no concept of writing. However, once they discovered writing, they could not undiscover it: the need for a system of writing was too great. The second option would be to acknowledge that Japanese could not be written down using Chinese characters, and to solve the problem by switching from speaking Japanese to speaking Chinese. The third option was to create a hybrid written language, based on Chinese characters combined with a phonetic 'alphabet' to record case endings, tenses and so on.

Adopting the Chinese language

The third option was the one that has eventually evolved, but not without the Japanese court at first trying option two. For many years in the fifth and sixth centuries AD, there seems to have been a concerted effort by the Japanese court to speak, write and read only Chinese. However, there was one fundamental flaw in the plan: the rest of the Japanese population, blissfully ignorant of the advantages of reading and writing, carried on speaking in Japanese. This meant that the court had to use the native tongue when dealing with the farmers, artisans and merchants who lived outside the court and who supplied food, clothing and all other necessities of life to the imperial retinue. So the experiment of using nothing but an imported language was dropped, but not until a vast number of words had been brought permanently into the Japanese vocabulary and a vast change made to the native language.

Connections with Chinese

Japanese today is grammatically unique, but in its vocabulary there are now many obvious connections with Chinese. They should not be overstated, because this huge importation of Chinese words happened at least 500 years before English imported many French words after the Norman Conquest, and today the English and French languages are entirely distinct. Japanese and Chinese, having no common grammatical heritage, are far more different from each other than English and French.

The Sinification of Japanese has complicated the vocabulary very much. That simple character meaning 'sun' can now be pronounced in four or five different ways, depending on the usage and meaning. Originally, there was just one Japanese word, pronounced *hi*, meaning 'sun', and by extension 'day'. The Chinese missionaries pronounced that character differently, so there are now two further pronunciations of the character, derived from different strains of Chinese: *nichi* and *jitsu*. There is also *ka*, which is a suffix for counting days (don't ask), as in the town name *Yokkaichi*, meaning 'Four Day Market'.

The next question is, how do you know when to pronounce the character *hi*, when is it *jitsu* and when is it *nichi*? Well, there is no hard and fast rule – it is all a matter of usage. When you are talking of the sun in the sky, then the pronunciation is *hi*. *Hi wa kyo tsuyoi desu* means 'The sun is strong today'. In compound words, a Chinese pronunciation is generally used. 'Sunday' is *nichiyobi*, the *nichi* and the *bi* parts of the word both being written with the same character. 'Yesterday' is *sakujitsu*, making use of the *jitsu* pronunciation. *Sakunichi* would be wrong, but there's no real logic to it.

The complexities of learning Japanese

The point of all this is not simply to confuse: it is to show what an ordeal the learning of the language can be. For most Westerners, learning to read and write involves learning an alphabet of 26 letters (or thereabouts) in upper and lower case, ten numerals from 0 to 9, plus a few accents and other punctuation marks. The entire body of English literature, every washing machine instruction manual and even the *Daily Mirror* can be read by anybody who has mastered no more than 70 or 80 different hieroglyphics. Because they are phonetic, it is possible to pronounce words without knowing their meaning, and with only 26 letters to choose from, looking up the meaning in a dictionary is simple enough. It's really not that difficult to learn to read and write English. Even a six year old could do it.

Japanese, on the other hand, requires a huge effort. Each character is different, and not necessarily connected to other characters of a similar shape either by pronunciation or meaning. So 日 is, as we have seen, *hi* or *nichi* or *jitsu* meaning 'sun' or 'day' but a similar character: 目 with one more brush stroke on top, is pronounced *haku* or *byaku* or *shiro* and means 'white'. Every character must therefore be learned separately, and in the absence of any logic, each one must be learnt purely by rote.

There are not, of course, just 26 characters, any more than English consists of just 26 words. My standard Japanese-English character dictionary contains 5,446 different characters, and that is merely for foreign students of the language. A Japanese dictionary for native speakers would contain many more. Imagine if you have to learn to read and write over 5,000 different pictures (for that in essence is what they are), none of which have any logical way of being sorted by meaning, pronunciation or way of writing. It is a mountainous task, a huge feat of determination and memory, but one which every Japanese schoolchild has to go through.

The process of learning to read and write Japanese

It is something that takes up much of every Japanese child's six years of elementary schooling, so that by the time they move on to their secondary schools, they are literate enough to write the essays and reports needed to study other subjects. They will by this time have mastered 881 basic characters (*kanji* = Chinese characters), and by the time they leave school, they must know and use 1,850 characters (plus about 100 more in common use in personal names) which will enable them to read all newspapers and magazines. They will also be masters of the two phonetic syllabaries, each containing 50 'letters', which the Japanese have devised to spell out the verb endings and other grammatical variations that so confused their ancestors. These syllabaries, known as *katakana* (カタカナ = square, or straightsided letters) and *hiragana* (ひらがな = cursive, or ordinary letters) are in everyday use and are the building blocks on which foreigners begin the daunting task of learning to read and write the language.

DON'T ASK WHY

Learning the language requires three characteristics in profusion: patience, an excellent visual memory and an acceptance of the way things are. It requires patience, coupled with determination and persistence, because learning to read and write is a long haul. This is another reason why patience is considered one of the highest virtues by the Japanese. It requires an excellent visual memory because without being able to retain the different images in the mind, and to recognise patterns within them, it would be impossible ever to become competent in written Japanese.

Most of all, it requires an unquestioning mind. A Japanese elementary school pupil is encouraged to ask 'how' – as in 'How do I write this character?' – and 'what' – as in 'What does this character mean?' – but never to ask 'why', – as in 'Why does this character look like this?' – because there is no answer to that question. There is, lost back in the mists of time, some connection between the shape of the characters and the shape of the thing they represent (the character meaning 'sun' is meant to be a picture of the sun with a wispy cloud floating across it, but it has become stylised to the point of unrecognisability), but modern Japanese characters cannot be worked out logically. The same can be said of the Western alphabet (Why is an 'a' shaped like that?) but with only 26 illogical shapes to deal with, there are still plenty of other entirely reasonable questions to be asked.

You might want to suggest at this stage that if Japanese can be written phonetically with two 50-character syllabaries, why don't they throw out the characters altogether and make the whole learning process much easier? Well, this solution has been thought of, as has the idea of using the western alphabet to write Japanese, which can be done, as it can with Chinese or Arabic. However, Japanese words are on the whole so short that many sounds have multiple meanings, and are only distinguishable by the way they are written. So, for example, the sound 'ka' has 15 different meanings, not counting 'the sound made by a crow', which strictly speaking is 'kaa'. These meanings range from the interrogative particle, the sound that comes at the end of every question, to 'mosquito', 'smell', 'frame', 'minority' and 'a load for a man', among others.

It is not unusual to see Japanese outlining the shapes of characters with their fingers as they talk, in order to make clear exactly what they are talking about. Japanese is full of puns and similar words which would cause total confusion if characters were abolished. *Kisha wa kisha de kisha shimashita* is a perfectly sensible sentence using the word *kisha* three times with three entirely different meanings. The translation is 'The reporter returned to his office by train'. *Kisha* can mean 'reporter', 'steam train' and 'returning to the office', depending on which characters are employed.

The end result of having to spend the best part of six years learning to read and write is that the Japanese do not learn to ask the question 'why'. They acquire brilliant retentive memories for the assimilation of facts, and incidentally the spatial awareness developed by the effort of learning all those different shapes helps a great deal in mathematics, but they do not learn to ask 'why'.

And if children up to the age of ten or 11 are not encouraged to ask why, you can be sure that as they grow older, they will not develop the habit either. The straitjacket imposed by the need to learn the language means that Japanese people are, as a general rule, great with facts but not so good at drawing conclusions from the facts. In business, if you ask a Japanese colleague, 'What do you think about this problem?' you will be greeted with a startled stare. If you ask, 'What do you know about this problem?', you will be given all the facts that could possibly be relevant, along with many that are not.

This is not to say that all Japanese are unable to draw conclusions from a set of facts, merely that their educational system does not encourage freedom of thought. This is in many cases a great strength: too many Western people believe that they should have their own opinion about everything, regardless of the facts. The Japanese preference for facts over opinions usually stands them in very good stead.

PRONUNCIATION

Japanese is a simple language to pronounce. There are only five vowel sounds, all of which are short. They are 'a', as in 'pat'; 'i', as in 'pit'; 'u', as in 'put'; 'e', as in 'pet'; and 'o', as in 'pot'. Sometimes the vowels are doubled, to lengthen them, but the basic sound remains the same. The only thing that changes is the length of time the sound is held. So *kyo*, meaning 'today' is pronounced with a long 'o'. You still keep you mouth in the same shape, but double the length of time, which makes the word sound as though it rhymes with 'roar'. Japanese has none of the impure vowel sounds of English.

The Japanese language works in syllables, not letters, so that every syllable ends with a vowel sound or – the one exception – an 'n' sound. All Japanese words, therefore, when transliterated into the western alphabet, end either with a vowel or the letter 'n'. They also do not use some of the consonant/vowel combinations we use, such as 'ti' (which becomes 'chi' in Japanese) and 'si', (which becomes 'shi').

And there is the problem, to western ears, of the 'l' and 'r' sounds. The Japanese 'l'/'r' is always transliterated as an 'r', but the sound is in truth halfway between 'r' and 'l', with a touch of 'd' in there as well. It is a difficult sound to master. If you put your tongue at the top of your mouth as though you were going to say a word beginning with 'd', and then say an 'r' word instead, you will be getting close to the sound of the Japanese 'r'.

LEVELS OF POLITENESS

We need to add two further complications to the Japanese language, which cause confusion to unwary foreigners. The first is that there are many levels of politeness within the Japanese language which are very difficult to get right. A boss, for example, will use different words when asking a subordinate to do something than the subordinate will use to express acceptance of the task. A man will use different words from those used by a woman, and an adult will use different words when dealing with a child. The verb endings are different, and the words to describe oneself and the person one is addressing will vary. So there are several words for 'I', depending on the status of speaker and addressee. *Watakushi* is the most commonly used word for 'I' (or although even more commonly it is left out altogether and merely understood), but there is also *watashi, ore, boku, ware* and no doubt several others.

When addressing anybody, it is polite to give a Japanese the honorific suffix -*san*, as in *Tanaka-san*, (which means Mr, Mrs or Miss Tanaka) but there are several other suffixes that Japanese will use as the occasion requires. -*Sama* is even more polite that -*san*, but is only normally used ceremonially; then there's -*kun* for people who are your juniors, -*sensei* for people who deserve particular respect (the word literally means 'teacher'), and -*chan* for children. Westerners should stick to -*san* tacked on to the end of the surname: that way you can't go wrong.

If your Japanese skills develop to the level where you can conduct conversations in the language, stick to the neutral polite forms: remember what we said about relationships and remember that the Japanese for a foreigner, *gaijin*, literally means an outsider. Try to avoid words that imply a particular relationship, whether upwards or downwards, with your listeners.

YES AND NO: NO AND YES

The second complication is the use of the words 'yes' and 'no'. The words 'yes' and 'no' give more difficulties in communications between Japanese and Westerners than any others. The reason is simple: to Japanese, 'yes' does not necessarily mean 'yes', and 'no' very rarely means 'no'.

When yes doesn't mean yes

The Japanese word you will find in the dictionary as meaning 'yes' is *hai*. But *hai* does not really mean 'yes'. It means, 'I have heard you, I have understood you, and I am now thinking of a reply'. So if a Japanese says *hai* in response to your question, 'Will you place an order for one million widgets at $10 each?' he does not mean that he has solved your factory's overproduction problems with one word. He has merely heard your question, and is probably thinking of a way to say 'no' without causing you to lose face. Even if he uses the word 'yes' in English, you must remember that his dictionary also says that the English for *hai* is 'yes', and he is merely using your language to indicate that he has heard, understood and is thinking of a reply. As Geert Hofstede points out, 'the word "yes" should not necessarily be seen as an approval, but as a maintenance of the communication line'.

I was told by one wise Japanese that the exact equivalent of *hai* is 'uh-huh'. 'Uh-huh' signifies nothing more that than you are still listening, and depending on the expression used can vary from absolute agreement to complete scepticism. *Hai* is very similar. So never assume that you have agreement when you hear the word 'yes' in discussion with a Japanese. If you need to be reassured that there is agreement, then ask a follow-up question, which requires an answer other than 'yes'.

'Will you deliver this by tomorrow?'
'Yes.'
'So what time tomorrow shall I expect you?'

This will prompt either a 'Sorry, I cannot do it tomorrow' or a 'Half past three', and then you will know what the 'yes' really meant.

The absence of no

The Japanese for 'no' is *iie*. But you will never hear this word used, except late at night in a bar when a Japanese reveller is being offered his umpteenth beer or whisky by his host, and has to admit that enough is enough. In this case, *Iie* means, 'I cannot possibly impose on any more of your kindness and hospitality. I won't have another beer/whisky.' The word for 'no' as in 'No, I won't buy a million of your lousy widgets' does not exist. 'No' is a confrontation.

Learning how to identify when a Japanese is saying no is one of the most difficult of all cross-cultural skills to acquire. There is no hard and fast rule which will help you – it's just a matter of experience. The Japanese phrase, *Saa, muzukashii desu ne!* ('Well, that's very difficult'), usually spoken after a sharp intake of breath between clenched teeth, is a pretty sure sign that what you have asked for is impossible, but of course, it is not the done thing to admit that what has been requested cannot be done. So the usual first word used to say 'no' is, inevitably, *hai*. If it is followed by a sucking of teeth, then you know that the 'yes' means 'no'. Another phrase that implies a strong negative is *kangaete okimasu* – literally, 'I'll think about it.' When a Japanese hears *kangaete okimasu*, he concludes the cause is hopeless. When he says, in English, 'I'll think it over', he is also stating as clearly as he can that the answer is no. But native English speakers are quite likely to keep on hoping when they hear that phrase.

My favourite 'no' is 'You may be right'. 'Yes, there was theoretically a chance that you could have been right, but actually you are totally wrong' is what it really means.

The idiosyncrasies of English
When speaking English with Japanese people, indeed with any non-native English speakers, it is essential to remember that the English we speak at home is a very colloquial language, a very indirect language and a language full of things understood or

implied but not actually spoken. English has two further idiosyncrasies in that native speakers use irony a great deal, and they use the negative in questions. Both these verbal quirks tend to baffle non-native speakers.

I remember one Japanese businessman who visited a British company on a day when the weather was terrible. It rained heavily all day and there was a strong wind to make it even more unpleasant. On reaching the company chairman's office, having had to sprint through puddles in the car park while our ineffectual umbrellas were blown about in the wind, the visitor tried to straighten his tie and hair from the ravages of the elements. The chairman, business cards in hand, greeted his guest in the approved manner, and then began his small talk with the statement, 'Isn't it a lovely day today!'

This caused complete confusion for his visitor, whose English was rudimentary (although much better than the British chairman's Japanese). In his opinion it was definitely not a lovely day, but then again, perhaps there had been a severe drought over the past few months in this part of Britain, so a torrential downpour could be interpreted as 'a lovely day'. So was the answer 'Yes' or 'No'?

Then again, because the question had been asked in the negative, in Japanese logic the answer should be either, 'Yes, it isn't a lovely day,' or 'No, it is a lovely day,' – the exact opposite of the technically illogical English usage. So the Japanese visitor did not know what the answer should be, and even if he did, he did not know how to reply in English. In the end, he just mumbled and took a sip of tea, and the meeting stumbled on for another 20 minutes or so, before he was released and allowed to go about his business.

Keep it simple

Don't use irony, don't use negative questions, and while we are about it, don't use idioms ('That's a completely different kettle of fish' once stopped a meeting for about half an hour's surreal explanation about haddock, cups of tea and how the saying has nothing to do with either). Keep your English as simple and direct as it realistically can be. Don't worry about vocabulary, although clearly jargon should be avoided. It's the grammar that confuses more than the words.

BODY LANGUAGE

Japanese body language is another cause for confusion. A great deal of any message is conveyed by means of gestures, emphasis and posture, and within European cultures we are broadly able to interpret how well the words fit the actions, so that we can judge the sincerity of the message being given. Japanese, and indeed all East Asian cultures, tend to have far less extravagant body language than western, especially southern European, cultures. This makes it very hard for a Westerner to work out what the true feelings of his Japanese counterpart are, and often lead to confusion when there is an apparent contradiction between the words and the gestures.

Eye contact

There are a handful of rules to remember when using and watching body language. Firstly, avoid direct eye contact. In the West, we consider it a sign of honesty if a speaker looks us in the eye, but in Japan people are very uneasy about any direct eye contact, even if for a short while. When giving a presentation, for example, Japanese people tend to look at the slides or their notes rather than the speaker, and even in a small business meeting, this will tend to be the case. You will often notice that people have their eyes shut in a meeting: this is not because they have fallen asleep (although very occasionally it might be), but because they can thereby avoid direct eye contact. It is also worth noting that because Japanese body language is so contained, it is not really necessary to look at a speaker to work out whether or not he is being sincere. So Japanese don't look at the speaker – they listen intently to the words, which can also be done more effectively with eyes shut.

Silence

Secondly, be aware of silence. Westerners are frightened by silence. In a business meeting, anything more than a couple of seconds' silence is interpreted as a potential disaster. Somebody did not understand something, or somebody does not like what I'm saying: I've shocked them into silence. The Japanese do not work like that. They consider it a remarkable skill that Europeans can listen and think at the same time, thus eliminating the need for silent thinking time. Japanese will listen until you stop speaking, and then take time to consider their response.

The almost irresistible impulse for any Westerner is to fill the silence with words, any words. The trouble is that once you have said all that you wanted to say, anything you add just to fill a gap in the silence is likely to weaken your case rather than strengthen it. So if you've said all you want to say and it's their turn to say something, keep quiet until they speak. It can be very difficult – ten seconds is a very long time to keep silent in a business meeting.

Your language or mine?

Language difficulties arise in dealing with any foreign culture, and with Japan the problems are no worse than with any other culture – nor indeed worse than foreigners encounter when dealing with the Brits. Remember the former German Chancellor Schmidt's dictum, 'When I am selling to you British, we will speak English, but when you are selling to me, *dann müssen wir Deutsch sprechen.*' Never go into a business meeting without somebody who can speak Japanese – it would be arrogant and impolite to do so. But equally, never assume that your own Japanese will be good enough to conclude a deal in the language: it won't be.

6

The Japanese Economy

Japan's economy is the largest in Asia, and second only to the United States in terms of national GNP. It is by far the dominant economy in East Asia, despite the phenomenal growth rates of the Chinese economy in recent years. The Japanese not only have the largest home economy, they are also the biggest foreign investor in almost every other East Asian economy, and their ships, insurance companies and freight agents dominate the actual transportation of goods around the region.

A MAJOR GLOBAL ECONOMY

Japan is by no means merely a regional power. Japanese companies have subsidiaries and joint ventures all over the globe, and it is hard to think of an industry, with the possible exception of the Yorkshire pudding industry or Dutch clog manufacturing, in which the Japanese are not significant players, either as suppliers, customers or competitors. If you are involved in anything but the most parochial of businesses, you need to be aware of what the Japanese are up to.

THE POST-WAR YEARS

In the years immediately after the Second World War, the Japanese economy grew at an unprecedented rate. This was caused by a variety of events all coming together at the same time. For a start, the economy could hardly have been at a lower level than it was in 1945. Japan's people had been sucked dry economically by over a decade of war, which had not only involved high taxation to pay for the war effort, but had also taken out of the productive economy hundreds of thousands of young men who would normally have been the driving force of the economy. Then, in the latter years of the war, the country had been ravaged by bombing that had laid waste the main cities, destroying factories, homes and good agricultural land. In August 1945, there was no Japanese economy to speak of.

American aid

However, for the Americans in the immediate post-war period, it was essential that Japan was a strong and loyal bastion against the Communist threat which was especially active in East Asia. From China, the Soviet Union and Korea, Communism was threatening to take over most of South and East Asia. Japan, occupied and defeated though she was, had to stand up against this threat. So the American occupation pursued a very enlightened and liberal series of policies to help the Japanese climb out of the economic pit they had created. They encouraged free trade, they helped them build their industries and – most importantly – they gave their struggling economy business to carry out.

QUALITY CIRCLES

Perhaps the decision that most shaped the Japanese economy in the post-war years was not made by the Americans, nor even by the Japanese authorities. In the first years of reconstruction, the Japanese went back to the methods they had employed to make their first great leap into western ways in the 1870s. They sought advice from the foreign experts. One man who was invited to speak initially at a trades union meeting in the late 1940s (as second or third choice, so legend has it), was the American quality control expert W E Deming. His talk was scarcely publicised and was not expected to mean much to the Japanese, but he was an expert and they wanted to hear what the experts thought.

Had they but known it, Deming at the time was hardly known in his native land. His radical ideas about putting quality first went against the grain in 1940s mass-production America, but in Japan he struck a powerful chord. His first series of lectures were a sensation, and the Japanese took up his ideas at once. He went on to give hundreds of lectures and seminars throughout Japan, often in sweltering factories in the heat of summer, on the necessity of statistical quality control. His ideas appealed exactly to the factual and numerate Japanese, and they put them quickly into action. As Deming himself said, 'I think I was the only man in Japan who believed my prediction in 1950 that within five years manufacturers all over the world would be screaming for protection. I think it took four years!'

Factory managers in Japan spent practically all their working days on the factory floor, not cocooned in some comfortable office like their western counterparts. They also encouraged the workforce to create teams dedicated to improving quality, a process which worked well in Japan where the group takes responsibility for everything, good and bad, and does not seek out individuals to praise or blame. Within a few years, the Japanese reputation for quality won them new customers, which in turn meant that with more orders to fulfil they could reduce prices. The post-war manufacturing boom in Japan was under way.

KEIRETSU AND ZAIBATSU

The other post-war decision that had the most effect on Japanese economic growth in the 1950s and 1960s was more a matter of luck than good judgement. The Americans had been impressed by the ability of Japan to build such a close knit economy that it was able to create the industrial and military machine that enabled it to go to war in the first place. In order to stop this happening again, they first of all wrote into the new Japanese constitution a clause stating that Japan would henceforth renounce war and would never even muster a standing army, navy or air force.

To make sure that this new peace constitution would stay in place, they also took a decision that they imagined would break up the financial and industrial powerhouses of the pre-war economy – the so-called *zaibatsu* (財閥) – without whom Japan would never again have the economic muscle to be tempted into war again. These *zaibatsu* were giants, like Mitsubishi, Mitsui, Sumitomo and Yasuda, vast conglomerates with interests in everything from shipbuilding to hotels and from insurance to banking.

The banning of holding companies

The American edict was a simple one: from now on, holding companies would be made illegal. A holding company is a company that exists purely to own another company or companies, and this type of structure is common enough in the West, as it was in pre-war Japan. By banning holding companies, the Americans thought they would break up the *zaibatsu* at a stroke, and the individual companies formerly owned by the holding company at the top would float free and flourish as independent units.

The success of this policy can be attested by the fact that the names of Mitsubishi, Mitsui and so on are as familiar and powerful, or indeed more familiar and powerful, as they were 60 years ago. The American policy was followed precisely, to the extent that holding companies were only made legal entities once again in Japan at the turn of the twenty-first century (when the economy slowed to a standstill and drastic measures were required to try to start it again). But the Americans reckoned without the Japanese primal urge for relationship building and mutual security. In place of the *zaibatsu* grew the *keiretsu* (径列) groups that were even better adapted to the economic realities of the post-war period than the old-fashioned *zaibatsu*. By the mid-1970s and through to the end of the 1980s, the *keiretsu* groups between them controlled about one quarter of Japan's economy, very much the same proportion as the old *zaibatsu* controlled before the war.

A way round the problem

Zaibatsu means, roughly 'financial group'. *Keiretsu* means, roughly, 'financial group'. The main difference between the two is that while the *zaibatsu* were a hierarchical group with a chairman at the top and a regular cascade of directors and managers, all in their right places on the rungs below, the *keiretsu* are groups of companies, each with interconnecting shareholdings and often with a common name, who do not have a main board at the top to direct policy. Obviously not – that would be illegal.

So the Mitsubishi group, for example, in its glory years from the mid-fifties to the mid-nineties, was a tightly woven spider's web of interconnecting companies, each of whom owned a small percentage of the other. There was no overall board running the whole group, but because they each owned a little bit of each other (including the Mitsubishi Bank), they all naturally helped each other and kept internal competition to a minimum. Of course, it would have been against the law to set up price fixing cartels or to purchase on the basis of special pricing for companies within the group, but the power of the relationship should not be underestimated.

Each *keiretsu* had an informal group of chief executives of the leading companies in the group (such as the Mitsubishi group's *Kinyokai*, literally, 'the Friday Club') who would meet regularly to play golf or drink sake but not, heaven forbid, ever discuss business matters unless they happened to crop up purely by chance as they topped up their glasses at the 19th hole. This way the leading players in any *keiretsu* could keep an eye on the direction the group was heading, which new products and new markets were looking likely to succeed and which to fail. They could also watch for unnecessary internal competition, and look at ways of co-operating on major projects. Because there was no edict from above ordering them to work together, the voluntary nature of the relationship was all the stronger.

Group identity

This system worked very well as the economy grew relentlessly for three decades and more. Group loyalty was established, a strong sense of group identity and of 'the Mitsubishi way of doing things' or 'the Sumitomo style' was engendered, and the *keiretsu* prospered. However, the system also relied to a great extent on continuing favourable world market conditions and a close and mutually supportive relationship with the government, most notably with the bureaucrats at MITI, the old Ministry of International Trade and Industry, which wielded a huge power to direct the economy, or at least the manufacturing and trading parts of it.

The disadvantages of the *Keiretsu* system

When things began to go wrong in the late 1980s, the flaws in the *keiretsu* system were quickly revealed. Because the cross-hatching of shareholdings had meant that it was almost impossible to tell who actually owned what percentage of which *keiretsu* company, they were in effect immune from takeover. It is a fact that until the very end of the twentieth century, no hostile takeover bid had succeeded in Japan, and even now they are virtually unheard of.

Being immune from takeover is good in many ways – it allows you the luxury of looking further ahead, of investing for the future and not worrying too much about short term returns – but it also meant that too many companies had not had their real worth tested in the financial markets for too long. Companies had over the years been supporting each other with little thought about the real worth of the business. When the banks, which were of course part of the same *keiretsu* and shareholders in the companies they were lending to, gave virtually unsecured loans on the basis of future business prospects rather than on real corporate worth, the potential was there for disaster if markets took a downturn.

And markets did take a downturn. The banks found they had made loans on the basis of unsecured future business, or vastly overvalued real estate, which now the borrowers could not repay. One economist even calculated at the end of the 1980s that the total book value of real estate in Tokyo alone, as shown in the annual reports of the top Nikkei-quoted firms in Japan, was greater than the total book value of all real estate in the United States, from New York to Los Angeles and all points in between. Clearly something was dangerously out of kilter.

A vicious circle

The banks were caught in a vicious circle: either they could bankrupt the companies they had lent to, and thereby give up all hope of getting their money back, or they could carry on lending even more in the hope that business conditions would turn around. Too many banks, knowing that their clients were also friends with whom they had enjoyed a long and profitable business relationship, chose the second option, and merely increased the bad debt potential. By the mid-1990s, Japan's indebtedness had grown way out of hand, and there was not the business to service the debts, let alone pay back the principal. The only way out was a huge reorganisation of the economy, with enforced mergers, bankruptcies and significant personal misery.

THE GOLDEN RECESSION

Japan in the early 1990s slipped into what has become known as 'The Golden Recession'. It was a recession in statistical terms, in that the economy shrank, or at least failed to grow, over a significant number of quarters, and as soon as it looked as though the corner might be being turned, another poor set of statistics were produced which knocked any talk of revival on the head.

The key to the solution, it seemed to all outside observers, was a reform of the banking system so that these huge unsecured loans would be a thing of the past. The trouble with that policy was that it would inevitably cause bankruptcies and job losses as the economy was shaken and reshaped to take into account the realities of *fin de siècle* world economics. Job losses were anathema to Japan's way of doing business: the economy had been growing for the entire working lives of everybody now facing up to the problems, and nobody had ever had to be laid off involuntarily within the heart of Japan's huge business engines, the *keiretsu*.

A challenge to the LDP government

The Japanese government was not really up to the task. For all but a few months of the post-war period, the ruling party has been the Liberal Democratic Party (known as the LDP, or *Jiminto*, 自由民主党 in Japanese). To be strictly accurate, until 1955 they were two different parties, the Liberal Party and the Democratic Party, who then merged, but between them they have held the reins of power for practically all the post-war period. The Liberal Democratic Party is, nominally at least, like the Holy Roman Empire, which was described as perfectly named except that it was not Holy, nor Roman, nor an Empire. The LDP is not Liberal (it is right-wing conservative), it is not Democratic (most of the key decisions are still taken behind closed doors in smoked filled rooms) and it is not a Party, but a loose collaboration of rival factions who disagree on almost everything except the need to cling on to power.

The LDP is the party of big business. The government has for many years worked hand in hand with big business, guiding the direction that industries took, protecting their home markets from foreign competition but encouraging ruthless internal competition among Japanese companies, and creating an environment that rewarded business endeavour. Japan thrived on this type of government, even though foreign competitors complained.

A closed market?

It has to be admitted that many of the complaints against Japan, certainly on the subject of the difficulty of selling into Japan, tended to be misguided. Japan was not, from the late 1960s on, a closed market at all. In fact, it was probably through the final quarter of the last century one of the most open markets in the world, more open than Europe or the United States.

The problem was that the rest of the world expected that their standard products would do for the Japanese market, and became upset when Japanese consumers rejected them. Whether we are talking about left-hand drive American cars or jars of British marmalade measured in pounds and ounces, foreign exporters were slow to grasp the particular needs of the Japanese market, and tended to expend their efforts elsewhere, while keeping up the complaints as a matter of routine. Sometimes they were justified, as when the Japanese attempted to keep Rossignol skis out of Japan on the basis that Japan had its own unique type of snow, but most of the time the problem was a failure to adapt to the local market. There were many success stories during this period, from IBM to Coca-Cola to Johnnie Walker whisky and Beatrix Potter branded tableware, but there were also a lot of failures.

You scratch my back...

Japan certainly did not help her own cause by allowing the intensely close relationships between government and industry to prosper. Civil servants, on reaching retirement age, were frequently appointed to the boards of corporations they had helped to regulate just a week or two earlier, a process known in Japan as *amakudari* (天下り) or 'descending from heaven'. The ex-bureaucrats appointed as directors or advisers would hold meetings with the men who had taken their place in the Ministry, and because the ex-bureaucrat had been senior to the people he was now dealing with from the other side, he would always tend to get his way. His new employers benefited, he benefited and even the people working their way up the ministry benefited, because they could see what enticements would be coming their way in a few years' time. It was a very cosy system and it worked.

Changes and a long recovery

When circumstances changed, however, the relationship between the government and industry was one of the first casualties. Due largely to external pressure which, being *soto*, is not something the Japanese have ever willingly given way to, the major players in Japan's economy began changing. The opening of the Japanese stock market to electronic dealing – Tokyo's Big Bang – in the early 90s brought a result that had not been expected locally. Instead of an influx of foreign investors eager to get on board the Japanese miracle train, a large number of passengers promptly disembarked and invested their money elsewhere, in Europe and America. Japan was clearly seen as a place not to invest, and the government had to find ways to get the economy running again.

The long recovery is another symptom of Japan's determination to stick with a plan until long after the whole thing has been shown not to work. There was from the beginning an extreme reluctance within Japan to do anything but tinker slightly with conditions. Big corporations were repeatedly saved from bankruptcy in order to safeguard jobs and reputations (not necessarily in that order) and a succession of prime ministers and finance ministers all promised radical action, which even if actually proposed was soon knocked down by the powerful vested interests in banking, finance and industry.

Of course, throughout this decade of economic stagnation, Japan has not looked like a country in an economic pit. Or at least, Tokyo has not looked like it. Unemployment, according to official figures, barely climbed above 5%, although official figures in Japan should never be believed except as an indicator of the direction the economy is going. Japan's positive trade balance rarely dipped below $100 billion, and the yen did not weaken to any significant extent. The stock market collapsed, certainly, to the extent that even after a 20% gain for the Nikkei index in 2003, the market was still at barely one quarter of its record high. To suggest that the value of Japanese business has been cut in four in the past decade is obviously wrong: the record high was massively overvalued, the present conditions are somewhat undervalued.

INVEST IN JAPAN

Many people have argued since the mid-1990s that Japan is a place to invest in, and quick. One of the problems during the boom years was that Japan became an incredibly expensive place. Rents went into orbit, and salaries were higher than the norm in the West. The result was that foreign firms were reluctant to set up offices and factories in Japan, and many who had tried joint ventures in the past had come away with horror stories about the different approach to a joint venture between East and West. (One might have thought that would be self-evident even before going into a joint venture, but to many Western businessmen it came as an unpleasant shock. It did to their Japanese partners too.)

Japan is still a very expensive country, but comparatively, it is much cheaper than it was in the 1980s. Rents and real estate prices have tumbled, but most significantly there is a skilled workforce available to any new company setting up, and this is the first time we can say that with confidence.

Recruitment problems

In the 1970s and 1980s, any foreign business coming to Japan faced a huge problem of recruitment. The Japanese system of lifetime employment, although it is exaggerated in western eyes, is nevertheless the stated aim of every white collar worker, and of every management in Japan. The result of this used to be that recruiting good Japanese staff at middle management level was almost impossible. It was always possible to find young people fresh from university to join a new company (although even then the big corporations and the civil service always got the pick of the graduates) and it was always possible to recruit senior 'advisers', semi-retired men who could build new business relationships for the new company. But it was always very difficult to find good people aged between about 30 and 45, who would be the driving force behind the new company, the people who actually formed the plans and did the work of the new business. The only people on the job market in that age group used to be people who were so incompetent that even under the lifetime employment system they had been let go. That was not a great encouragement for businesses hoping to come to Japan.

The only viable alternative was to establish a joint venture, and recruit key people from the staff of the joint venture partner. This was not a particularly satisfactory solution either, as all too often the Japanese partners' staff were transferred to the new venture in name only, retaining their true loyalty to the parent company and working towards the day when they would be transferred back from the semi-foreign limbo in which they found themselves. If this sounds a little harsh, it only reflects the realities of very many joint ventures in the latter part of the last century: the Japanese do not transfer loyalty on demand.

A new career pattern

However, the Golden Recession has changed all this. For the first time, good middle managers have been laid off and find themselves on the labour market again, through no fault of their own. There are plenty of good people who feel that the Japanese industrial/ political complex has failed them, and they want to create their own career paths, much on the western model. While it would be an exaggeration to suggest that the ideal of lifetime employment is dying in Japan, there is a change being seen. We can certainly expect that over the next decade or so, the Japanese career pattern will begin more closely to resemble the western pattern.

THE JAPANESE WORKING WOMAN

One of the other advantages of this prolonged period of recession is the opportunity it has offered women. Japan is, as we have seen, a man's country, and women have struggled to gain for themselves any sort of valued place in the workforce. However, with their husbands often finding themselves out of work, Japanese women have been forced to find ways of bringing income to the family, while at the same time not shaming their husbands by being obviously the only breadwinner.

Female entrepreneurs

The result is that women are increasingly turning their backs on any hope of a career in a big corporation – which has in any case rejected their husbands – and are finding entrepreneurial ways of earning money. Increasingly we are noticing women setting up businesses, often with a man as the nominal chairman or chief executive to cater to Japanese sensitivities. Many of the brightest new companies in Japan, especially in those areas of the economy most obviously associated with women's interests, are run by women. The only raw material that Japan has is its people, and for too long they have been ignoring the 50 per cent who have been encouraged to find husbands, become housewives and raise children – and stay out of the mainstream economy. The Golden Recession is helping to change that. This may be good news for companies wanting to invest in Japan, but it must be bad news for Japan's competitors as this vast untapped resource comes onto the market.

Traditional values

The Japanese woman has long been ignored, especially by Japanese man. As one distinguished Japanese economist, and incidentally a woman, Noriko Hama has noted, 'Gender discrimination, male chauvinism and sexual harassment are accepted and tolerated.' The moral code is traditional: wives are expected to be subservient, quiet, modest and unflappable. Husbands can do as they please. In truth, this state of affairs is changing, but it is still the custom for everybody to wish to get married, and still the vast majority of people do.

Pressure to get married

This is in part as a result of family pressure. There is a sense that a person has 'failed' if they are not married by the age of 30, and families will do all they can to seek out a suitable partner for their son or daughter. Even in twenty-first century Japan, there are many arranged marriages where the bride and groom hardly know each other before they marry. People whose equivalents in the West would look upon a lifetime union with somebody of the opposite sex as their definition of hell, will nevertheless get married and produce the regulation two children, to satisfy social pressures. In their spare time they may act as they please: sexual fidelity has never been a definition of Japanese marriage as it is in Christian cultures.

Divorce

Divorce is becoming more common, but the rates are still well below those in the West. Young people are forgiven if they make one 'mistake' in the marriage stakes. For many, one divorce bestows an aura of sophistication. There is even the phenomenon of the *Narikon* as it is called: a couple who go off on honeymoon after a big ceremony, but before the legal registration of their union, discover they are incompatible after two weeks in each other's company. So they call it a day as their flight returns to Narita. *Rikon* is the Japanese for 'divorce'. A *Narikon* is a Narita divorce.

Marriage and children – a population problem

It is still very rare for a couple to live together before marriage, and only the bravest few would announce this fact to family or friends. Illegitimacy remains a stigma, and fewer than 2% of registered births in Japan are to unmarried parents. The family is still very much seen as the rock around which Japanese society is built, and the lack of immigrants bringing alternative marriage habits to the country means that the pace of change is not rapid.

The biggest problem facing Japan is the fact that the younger generation are not producing children at the rate their parents did. By 2007, it is estimated that the population will start shrinking, and in the second decade of the century, it is expected that Japan will have as many pensioners as workers, imposing a huge strain on the tax and welfare systems. It is this ageing of the population which is probably the biggest economic and social hurdle to overcome, and the one that must be addressed even before the Golden Recession is a thing of the past.

The Business World

Almost more than any nation, the Japanese have an international reputation for being businessmen. This is not meant to denigrate, like Napoleon's description of England as a nation of shopkeepers, but is merely a statement of the way the world perceives that Japan has built itself up again after the cataclysm of the Second World War. The Japanese *sarariman*, conservatively dressed in his dark blue suit, white shirt and dark tie, carrying the ubiquitous A4 size brown envelope, is as much a symbol of modern Japan as the *samurai* is a symbol of her past. But how do we deal with these people, and how do we build successful business relationships with them?

BASIC VALUES

In an exercise a few years ago, Japanese businessmen were asked to compile a list of the basic values of their society and western society, and of the typical management systems in each culture. The results were revealing, not only in what they say about their own culture, but also in the way they contrast it with 'western culture' (if such a thing exists).

Their list of the basic values of the cultures included such obvious points as an 'us' culture in Japan, contrasted with a 'me' culture in the West, with its natural corollaries such as community spirit as against individualism; the concept that talents belong to society in Japan, while they belong to the individual in the West; and the concept that personal promotion is not advisable in Japan but 'always the best' in the West.

Basic Values of Society

◈ Japanese

- ❖ COMMUNITY SPIRIT
- ❖ TALENTS BELONG TO SOCIETY
- ❖ MONEY IS SECONDARY
- ❖ PERSONAL MAXIMISATION IS NOT BEST
- ❖ RESPECT FOR OLD AGE
- ❖ HOMOGENEITY
- ❖ TACIT UNDERSTANDING
- ❖ AN 'US' CULTURE

◈ Western

- ❖ INDIVIDUALISM
- ❖ TALENTS BELONG TO THE INDIVIDUAL
- ❖ MONEY REFLECTS ACHIEVEMENT
- ❖ PERSONAL MAXIMISATION IS ALWAYS BEST
- ❖ RESPECT FOR YOUTH
- ❖ HETEROGENEITY
- ❖ LEGALISTIC SOCIETY
- ❖ A 'ME' CULTURE

FARNHAM CASTLE
INTERNATIONAL BRIEFING &
CONFERENCE CENTRE

FARNHAM CASTLE
INTERNATIONAL BRIEFING &
CONFERENCE CENTRE

Typical Management Systems

● Japanese

- ❖ LIFETIME EMPLOYMENT
- ❖ REWARD BY SENIORITY
- ❖ INFORMAL CONTROL
- ❖ VAGUE JOB DESCRIPTIONS
- ❖ GROUP RESPONSIBILITY
- ❖ SEPARATION OF RANK AND TASK
- ❖ EMPHASIS ON CO-ORDINATION AND CO-OPERATION
- ❖ CONSENSUS DECISIONS
- ❖ BOTTOM-UP MANAGEMENT
- ❖ NON-SPECIALISED CAREER PATH (ON THE JOB TRAINING)
- ❖ RECRUITMENT AT GRADUATE LEVEL
- ❖ NO PRESSURE ON PERFORMANCE

● Western

- ❖ SHORT-TERM EMPLOYMENT
- ❖ REWARD BY INDIVIDUAL PERFORMANCE
- ❖ FORMAL CONTROL
- ❖ EXPLICIT JOB DESCRIPTIONS
- ❖ INDIVIDUAL RESPONSIBILITY
- ❖ RANK DEFINES TASK
- ❖ EMPHASIS ON EFFICIENCY AND RESULTS
- ❖ INDIVIDUAL DECISIONS
- ❖ TOP-DOWN MANAGEMENT
- ❖ SPECIALISED CAREER PATH
- ❖ RECRUITMENT AT ALL LEVELS
- ❖ INTENSE PRESSURE ON CURRENT PERFORMANCE

These are views the Japanese have picked up through exposure to Hollywood movies as much as in business dealings, but the broad truths are inescapable: the Japanese are a homogenous group while Western societies are heterogeneous individuals trying to outdo each other.

TYPICAL MANAGEMENT SYSTEMS

Their list of typical management systems points up several key lessons for anybody who aspires to working efficiently with the Japanese. At the top of their list is the principle of lifetime employment, which as we have already seen, is being seriously dented by the Golden Recession. But if lifetime employment is beginning to become less common, it is still far more usual than in the West. A Japanese businessman will want to stay with the same company all his working life, even if he does not succeed in his goal. The Japanese view of Westerners is that we tend to move around from company to company, selling our services to the highest bidder: the individual view of life as opposed to the group view of life. Japanese people would say that this is why Westerners are so concerned with salary levels (as if Japanese workers are not) and tend to judge levels of excellence in monetary terms. 'I must be a better manager than you because I am earning more than you'. This is not a concept that the Japanese follow.

The fundamental importance of relationships

In dealing with Japanese people, it follows that if lifetime employment is the ideal, then loyalty to the company and being proud of the company you work for are key attributes in being successful. Japanese companies want to forge long-lasting business relationships, and these must be based around the people who represent the companies within the relationship. If they are given the impression by a potential partner that a particular individual is the only person to deal with, or that key members of the relationship teams are always moving on, then they will be very reluctant to enter into any sort of worthwhile business projects.

In European banks, as an example, there are frequently people with titles such as 'Relationship Manager' or 'Personal Banker', but these people move around just as frequently as anybody else in the highly impersonal world of financial services. Nobody in Japan would have a title like 'Relationship Manager': it would be self-evident to them that they all have a responsibility for managing, helping and building relationships throughout their working lives. Something like that is so fundamental to their business goals that it cannot be left to just one or two people who are called 'Relationship Managers'.

Job descriptions

Another item on the Japanese list of typical business systems is 'vague job descriptions' in Japan, with explicit job descriptions being the norm in the West. That's another reason why we have people called 'Relationship Managers': everybody has a precise role in the organisation and everybody needs to know what they are supposed to do. In the UK, a company cannot expect to qualify for the 'Investors In People' certification unless it has a comprehensive system of job descriptions and evaluation programmes for all employees. In Japan, the nearest most companies get to a job description is 'Do whatever the company asks you to do'. Even that is unlikely to be written down, but providing that what the company asks you to do is legal, nobody seems to mind. There are almost no trades unions in Japan, with strict demarcation lines over who should do what. Unions are company-wide. Every employee of a company is a member of the union, but no outsider is a member.

Rewarding seniority

The issue of rewarding seniority as opposed to rewarding performance is another key difference between Japan and the West. Once again, the extremes of disparity between East and West are beginning to disappear as companies all over the world take on multinational values, but the Confucian ethic of respect for age is still firmly embedded in the Japanese psyche. This means not only that, for instance, there is a national holiday on Respect For The Aged Day (15 September), but also that the virtues of experience and the wisdom that experience brings are highly valued.

In business terms, it is very common for a significant part of the monthly salary level to be calculated by years of service, rather than on individual achievement. In the 1970s, there was an example of a factory cleaner who had been with the company for 35 years earning more than the most successful salesman in the company, who had only been with them for three years. These types of example are increasingly hard to find nowadays, but the principle of respect, and therefore reward, for loyalty and longevity is still prevalent.

Separation of rank and task

One of the more difficult concepts to grasp about Japanese corporations is this idea of the separation of rank and task. In the West, a businessman's position defines his task. The production manager is responsible for production: he or she has a budget within which to work and a set of goals to achieve. Success or failure will be the production manager's personal responsibility. In Japan, rank and task are two separate things.

The hierarchy of the big Japanese corporations is very clearly defined. The titles that people have carry significance beyond the company and give authority that has no real connection to the ability of the person to do the job. It is a bit like the army. The rank of captain or general denotes a status within the organisation, but it does not in any way define the job that the captain or general actually does. One captain might be commanding tanks in the desert; another might be supervising the preparation of the staff officers' lunches.

Similarly, in Japan, the title of *bucho* (部長 = department chief) or *kacho* (課長 = section head) denotes a rank in the organisation, but does not actually define what the holder of the title does. These ranks, although having no legal status, are to be found in practically all companies in Japan, and enable a *kacho* in one company to talk to a *kacho* in another, knowing that they are of the same basic rank. It is always important to make sure that people who wish to talk business to each other are of similar rank: a managing director cannot do business with a mere section chief. The tasks that the section chief is responsible for are the tasks that his entire section is responsible for. While he may be the senior person, by service or age, in the section, he is not necessarily the driving force behind the section, nor even the 'leader' in western terms.

The separation of rank and task has a corollary – most Japanese managers follow a non-specialised career path, while we in the

West like to think of ourselves as specialists. If a Westerner meets somebody for the first time, in a pub or at a party for example, the question, 'What do you do?' will no doubt be asked. The average Westerner will answer, 'I'm an accountant,' or 'I'm a teacher' or 'I'm an airline pilot'. In response to the same question, a Japanese will say, 'I work for Mitsui' or 'I work for Sony.' The Westerner thinks of him- or herself as a specialist with a skill which some lucky organisation is getting the benefit of at the moment, but who may move on whenever they please.

A Westerner's business card will not only show his name, status and company name, but also his qualifications – BA (Hons), MA, PhD, M. Inst. Mech. Eng., MP, DFC and bar – the list is endless. Most Japanese business cards will show the bearer's company name, his status within the company and the usual company details. With the one regular exception of medical doctors, it is unusual for a Japanese to list his personal qualifications on a business card. It appears boastful, and anyway these skills are for the benefit of the company rather than of the individual.

Non-specialists

When a Japanese joins a company, he works in whatever position the company decides to put him in. It is not unusual for language graduates to be working in production engineering, or for physicists to be in the marketing department. A potential manager in a Japanese company will be transferred from department to department as he zigzags his way up the corporate ladder. A Western executive will begin at the bottom of his specialist department and work his way vertically up as the opportunity arises, but a Japanese will move from section to section, even when he has attained a very high rank. A big company will have a large number of these free-floating executives criss-crossing their organisation charts, a state of affairs that creates two distinct differences between Japanese and western corporations, however much their corporate organograms may appear to match.

The first difference is that the managers in a Japanese company are specialists, but not in the way we would understand it in the West. They are specialists in their own company: they know all the aspects of its work, they know its values and they know its people. Therefore they are instantly able to interpret the ways of their company to outsiders, and to act in a way that exactly conforms to its values. The company becomes far more 'high context', in cultural terms, than any western organisation, and communication is based more on people and their significance than on words alone. It is a state of affairs that few western companies would feel at ease with.

Understanding other departments

The second difference is that there is a general tendency for corporate politics to be less fractious in Japanese companies. When working in a British manufacturing company, I used to have to chair the monthly production planning meeting, when production always wanted to make what was easy to make, and sales wanted to have what was easy to sell. The two things were not always the same, and because our company, in common with most British companies, had bonus schemes for different parts of the company based on different criteria, there was little incentive for the two sides to reach agreement.

In Japan, on the other hand, a member of the sales team at that monthly meeting would know that he might well be transferred to the production department in the next few months, so any outcome that did not benefit both sides would be storing up trouble for him in the future. What is more, he would most probably have been part of the same team (even if it was in HR or accounts) as some of the people across the table at this meeting, so they would be good friends as well as colleagues. Agreement would be quickly reached.

The down side of this system only shows itself when things are not going well. The almost complete lack of new blood into an organisation means that bad habits do not get noticed, and in tough times it is the bad habits that bring an organisation down. In good times, though, the Japanese system merely supports and confirms an already successful structure. In the Golden Recession, more and more companies are beginning to appreciate the value of new blood to question old practices.

Pressure on performance

The final item on that list compiled by Japanese managers is the contrast between 'no pressure on performance' for Japanese workers, but 'intense pressure on current performance' for Westerners. This is, in my view, utterly untrue. The reason that the Japanese perceive the difference is that in the West we are all set individual targets, and the sales figures, production graphs and so on that abound in all offices are a constant reminder of whether or not we are achieving our own particular part of the project. It is simple to tell at any time whether or not any particular person is on target to succeed or fail, and to the Japanese, this is intense pressure. It is intense because it puts individuals in the spotlight, a place where most Japanese do not like to be.

However, we all know of many examples where a European salesman has achieved his annual targets with ten months of the year still to go: he has no pressure to help out his colleagues and so he is operating under no pressure at all. He might put himself under pressure to make it look as though his target was realistic rather than ridiculously understated, so that for the next year he also has a pressure-free target, but in general in the West, we do not work under intense pressure all the time.

In Japan, they do. This is because the individual is subordinate to the group, and it is the group's achievements that are measured. The individual within the group has two pressures: the first is to ensure that he does not let down the group by failing to perform his duties to the highest level (and this is a very strong moral pressure indeed); and the second is to help anybody in the group who for whatever reason is not performing well, so that the group still achieves its target. That in anybody's book (or in anybody from the West's book) is pressure. Suicide in Japan among median age office workers is higher than in the West, and in Japan they have even had to invent a new word: *karoshi* meaning 'death from overwork'.

BUSINESS ETIQUETTE

There are hundreds of books available that will tell you more about Japanese business etiquette than you wish to know. Every aspect of potential misunderstanding is brought under the microscope and dissected until it is unrecognisable. In reality, though, there are probably no more than three rules that will get you most of the way there: be on time, have plenty of business cards and don't let anybody lose face. To that we should add the cardinal virtues of patience and persistence, and a complete understanding of your own position, which are things you should bring with you to any meeting with any culture including your own.

Punctuality

Being on time is important. Because so much of what is done in Japan is the mask rather than the reality, the start of any relationship carries special significance. The Japanese like punctuality, and they also like face to face meetings. You will find that in Japan you spend much more time travelling from office to office for meetings than you do in the West. Arriving on time is a courtesy that must be followed. If a meeting is scheduled for 3 p.m., for example, people who know what city traffic can be like in Japan will give themselves plenty of leeway to arrive on time. As a result, the coffee shops in and around any major office block will be packed from about a quarter to the hour to five minutes to the hour, full of people killing time until they can make their way to the meeting, arriving at the reception desk no later than three minutes before the appointed time.

Formal meetings

Meetings in Japan are formal. You will meet in a designated meeting room, not in anybody's office, and the seating layout will always be the same: a table will confront you as you walk in to the room, with a window in the wall behind it. Nobody else will be there when you arrive: your hosts will turn up only when they are sure you are settled in with a cup of *ocha* (Japanese tea).

Visitors always sit on the side of the table facing the door, and the hosts will sit with their backs to the door. This custom apparently dates from feudal times when assassins were commonly prowling around. The host would always sit with his back to the door so that if an assassin burst in, the guests would see him first, and have a little time to draw their swords. The ever polite hosts would be hacked to pieces as they sat. This is a romantic idea, but as most assassins would have been paid by one party or the other, they knew who to attack whether they were facing the door or not. It must also be remembered that the inner walls of Japanese castles were *shoji*, made of ricepaper and balsa wood. Any sword sharp enough to cut a man's head off at a stroke would also have been sharp enough to cut through paper and balsa without any difficulty.

BUSINESS CARDS

When the hosts come into the room, the very first thing that happens is the exchange of business cards (名刺 = *meishi*). The business card is perhaps the most important tool in Japanese business. It is what identifies you, and it is the symbol of your relationship with your company. The collection of cards that any Japanese person accumulates becomes his address book, his telephone book and the index of his business relationships. It is therefore essential that you have a good stock of cards and that you give them out correctly.

There are one or two rules governing *meishi*. The first is that they should all be a standard size (91 × 55 mm) so that they fit into the plastic trays that every *sarariman* has in which to file his business cards. Too big, and they will never get into the file, too small and they will be lost among hundreds of others. Either way, your card will not be used again.

The second rule is that you must never give your card a second time to somebody you have already given it to, for that implies that you have forgotten the person concerned, a huge loss of face for all concerned. This can be difficult for visiting *gaijin* who only come to Japan once every six months or so, but in practice it is quite easy to stay clear of trouble. It is the custom for the host to give his card before the guest reciprocates, so that if you are not quite sure, but have not received one from your Japanese host, do not give one in return. He already knows you. If you are still insensitive enough to hand over your card, then best practice (if your solecism is pointed out) might be to suggest that your e-mail address or mobile phone number or something else on the card has changed since the last meeting. If you give your card to the same person two days in a row, then there is nothing to be done except to suggest you pay a little more attention to your hosts in future.

Business cards are handed over with both hands. If your hands are full of other people's cards, which makes offering yours with two hands a difficult prospect, it is OK to use just the right hand. But not the left hand. Using the left hand is basically impolite, although it must be admitted it is not as terrible a *faux pas* as it might be in Arab cultures or in Korea or Thailand, for example. However, all Japanese used to be (are often still are) trained from birth to be right-handed, and it is still very rare to come across a Japanese who writes left-handed. The percentage of left-handed foreigners is much higher, and you have to be careful about using your left hand too much.

I am left-handed, and soon discovered that if I were to try to use chopsticks right-handed, as recommended in the etiquette books, I would not only find myself with massive laundry and dry cleaning bills for my shirts and suits, but I would also in all probability starve within a few weeks of arriving in Japan. So I used my left hand instead. Because I was aware that left-handedness was improper, I would always ask permission of my companions at any meal to eat with my left hand – a permission that was never refused and which showed that to a small extent at least, this *gaijin* understood Japanese etiquette.

The final and in many ways most important thing to remember about business cards is that you must NEVER write on one in the presence of the person who gave it to you. Even if he says, 'Let me give you my home phone number,' you should not write this on his card. You must pass the card back to him so that he can write on it himself.

GIFTS GIVEN AND RECEIVED

One other aspect of the Japanese business meeting that worries non-Japanese is gift giving. The Japanese love presenting gifts to people, and the assumption among non-Japanese is that they are always going to have to give a gift to a Japanese contact. This is not really true, and it is important that you do not get caught in a spiral of ever more expensive gifts as one party feels an obligation to reciprocate – but just a tiny bit more expensively – for the latest gift received.

There are a few rules about Japanese gift giving that should be remembered. Firstly, there are two major gift-giving seasons in Japan, mid-summer and year end, called *ochugen* (summer) and *oseibo* (year end). It would not be normal to bring a gift to a business meeting at any other time of the year, unless there was a specific reason for it. However, all visitors to Japan should always bring their company's latest Report and Accounts, any relevant promotional material, brochures, samples, etc., as Japanese colleagues are always keen to have the maximum amount of information about anybody they work with.

What to give

The gifts that are given in Japan during the gift seasons are company to company rather than person to person, and therefore should not be too personal. Gifts are much more form than content, so the wrapping, for example, is often more important than the gift itself. A gift wrapped in Takashimaya Department Store paper, for example, will demonstrate that the giver has spared no expense in buying the gift, even if when it is opened up, it proves to be no more luxurious than, say, a face towel. The gift itself is almost always a practical item – soap, towels, cooking oil, beer and so on – and of little real value.

A British company should probably arm itself with something fairly inexpensive, peculiarly British and with some practical purpose, but not too personal to the giver or receiver: a Wedgwood ashtray, for example, or an illustrated book about Windsor Castle. There was a time when gifts could be very expensive, such as a gold watch or a crocodile handbag – but now that gifts of such value might be construed as bribes, you will not be on the receiving end of anything too costly. It is, however, very impolite indeed to refuse a gift, however much you may not want to accept yet another kilo of beautifully wrapped butter.

How and when to present a gift

Remember also that gifts are traditionally not opened in the presence of the giver. If you take a gift with you to a business meeting, it will be handed over at the end of the meeting. This is why all business gifts should be small enough to be kept inconspicuously in a briefcase: if the meeting goes badly, you never need to reveal that you even had a gift you were thinking about handing over. Your Japanese counterpart will thank you very sincerely for the gift, and immediately reciprocate, but neither of you should open the present there and then. If in doing so, you revealed by some slight involuntary twitch of a facial muscle that this was not the most splendid gift you had ever received, there would be huge loss of face all round. Much better to open the present quietly back at the office. Or even, as many Japanese do, just keep the present in its wrapping and hand it on unopened to the next person who deserves to be given a business gift.

LOSS OF FACE

Perhaps the most difficult thing for a foreigner to come to terms with in dealing with the Japanese is the issue of loss of face. It has been exaggerated to an extent that many people become over sensitive, but the issue is still very real. In essence, nobody – Eastern or Western – likes losing face, being made to look small or foolish in front of others. In Japan, however, this is taken to a greater extreme, so that nobody is ever put in a position where face might be lost.

The Japanese idea of the mask, and the real truth behind the mask, is so important that to have the mask damaged or stripped away – to lose face – is a great dishonour which can seriously compromise a person's effectiveness at work. Whereas in the West vigorous arguments about work issues are commonplace and do not usually descend to the personal level, in Japan there is a risk that even the mildest form of disagreement can be seen as an attack on another person's honour, with all the implications that brings.

We have already seen how the Japanese avoid having to say 'no', and indeed get the message across by saying 'yes' or 'you may be right'. In a group, the result of this reluctance to express a contrary opinion means that no controversial or even vaguely difficult issues can be discussed. Nobody is going to speak out about an issue for fear of causing unexpected difficulties for somebody else in the meeting. However much the production director may believe that his present problems are caused by the purchasing department's ridiculous cost-cutting efforts, he is not going to say so in a meeting where the sales director or chief accountant are also present, because he does not want the purchasing chief to lose face.

If a man causes another to lose face, then he loses face as well. And by extension, if others are present when a loss of face occurs, then they lose face too for having been powerless to stop the situation arising in the first place. So the situation does not arise. Ever. Things just do not get discussed in the way we discuss them in the West. Japanese meetings are to pass on information, not to reach decisions. They are for getting to know people and exchanging pleasantries, but they are not for raising difficult subjects. Visitors to Japan forget that at their peril.

8

Negotiating with the Japanese

In order to achieve any business success anywhere in the world, it is highly likely that negotiations have to take place. Negotiating with the Japanese is not totally different from any other sort of negotiations, and indeed the principles they follow are ones that we can easily work to, provided that we understand these principles in the first place. As we have already seen, the key to Japanese business style is the establishment of a firm relationship, and no serious negotiations can get under way until that relationship is in place. Japan is not a country where quick deals can be done, where you can offload your excess stock at a cheap price or expect to make good money from a one-off deal. The relationship is all.

ESTABLISHING A RELATIONSHIP

Establishing a relationship with any Japanese organisation requires the right introductions. You cannot just turn up on their doorstep and hope to sell your widgets, or indeed to buy their widgets. They must know who you are first. Even direct sales and telephone cold calls, which in Japan are a part of the economy if not quite so great as in many western countries, rely on a general awareness of the company offering the services and some attempt on their part to understand the needs of the potential consumer.

The Internet has certainly gone some way to breaking down the personal interface that people have long assumed is essential in dealing with the Japanese, but Internet sales in Japan are mainly limited to standard items such as books, air fares and some foodstuffs. Pizza and Chinese food delivery services thrive in Japan, but this is because of the personal service they offer: you can fax or e-mail your order through to the restaurant and they will send a man on a motorbike with your order to your apartment within minutes. They rely on a regular high quality service to bring in repeat business, to build a relationship with the customer even if he or she is only glimpsed briefly at the front door as the food is delivered. Once again we should note that in everything, quality counts. The lessons of W E Deming are still valid.

'Window' people

If you do not have the right introductions when you come to call on a new potential business partner, you may not reach the right people to talk to. Many Japanese companies still employ people who are known unofficially as *madogiwazoku* (窓際族 'the tribe beside the window'). These are the middle managers who may have started brightly in the company 20 years before, but who now have run out of steam. They may have a title such as *kacho* (section chief), but they are unlikely to have any real function or duties. Their role in the organisation now is to sit at their comfortable desks by the window, and spend the day checking that the car park is still there, or that nobody has stolen the coffee shop across the road. As soon as they reach the retirement age of 55, they are released. There may be fewer of these people in Japan these days, but they still exist. What's more, one of their main uses is to meet and greet visitors who are not important to the company.

You may therefore turn up for a first meeting and have an apparently very positive welcome from one of these people. He will be very interested to learn of your new products, services and price lists, but that is only because anything is more interesting than sitting looking out of the window all day. When he reports back to his colleagues, they will quickly decide that no further action should be taken, and you will be back to square one, or even worse. The only way to be sure that you will not meet one of these people when you first try to establish relations with a Japanese company is by having a go-between who can give you good introductions. You have to be brought into the web of Japanese corporate relations by somebody who is already within that web.

Getting to know each other

Assuming that you do get to sit down with the right people in the new company, what are the next steps? Well, the first part of any negotiation is the process of getting to know you. Your Japanese potential partner will look on the business relationship as a kind of marriage, which is for richer and for poorer and in sickness and in health till death do you part. It is not a quick one night stand. The first meetings and exchanges of information will cover the way your company works, the way you go about your business, your status in the local community and in your business sector, your reputation for quality and for trustworthiness. Your Japanese counterpart will also be happy to hand over to you information on all these topics, expecting you to want to know, in the words of the man in the film *Butch Cassidy and the Sundance Kid*, 'Who are these guys?'

Exchange of information

At this stage in the negotiations, you should be keen to show the Japanese round your factories and other sites, give them access to all non-confidential information and expect similar information in return. If you do not do this, the Japanese will find out anyway. This is their fact-gathering tendencies coming out, as well as their desire to avoid uncertainty: they want to know as much about you as possible before entering into the relationship so that there will be fewer surprises in the years ahead.

It is no good exaggerating either. If you have a market share of 5%, don't claim it is 15%. If you produce 500 widgets a day at your most efficient factory, don't pretend you can make 1000. Japanese sources of information are very reliable and they will discover the truth. Falsehoods and exaggerations will kill the relationship off before it has started. Whether the Japanese are intending to sell their products to you or you wish to sell to them, you can be sure that they will know a great deal about you even before the first approach is made.

BINDING THE ROOTS

To the Japanese, this is all part of the preparations for the negotiation process. They call it *nemawashi* (根回し) which literally means 'binding the roots'. In order to transplant rice seedlings from the nursery fields into the main paddy fields, the roots have to be bound up to enable them to survive the process. Thus *nemawashi* has come to mean the preparation before any major undertaking, and is used frequently in Japan, even when a Japanese is speaking in English. *Nemawashi* takes as long as it needs to take. There is no set time for the process to be deemed complete. Whereas a western company would set a time limit on concluding a contract, Japanese companies set no time limit on the process of reaching agreement.

The *nemawashi* will also form the major part of any final decision-making process. Remember also that for a Japanese company to enter into a relationship with you, they will probably have to break an existing relationship. It does not matter whether your product is cheaper, better quality, smaller or anything else: if another company is already supplying your potential client with the widgets you now intend to supply, a relationship must be broken off, or at least considerably reduced. This is a painful process, because it involves real people who might now find themselves struggling with empty order books, real people who have been part of a successful relationship for many years. There is virtually no shareholder pressure to do business simply on the financial criteria of price, quality and delivery as there would be in the West. Japanese companies will continue relationships with companies whose prices may not be the keenest simply because the relationship has worked until now.

Internal negotiation

Once a Japanese company has decided that your company is worth dealing with, they will then want to build consensus within their company about the way the relationship will work. This involves negotiating with everybody within the organisation who might be affected by the decision to work with you. If you are going to provide widgets as a component for one of their key products, for instance, then the people who need to be in agreement with the change of supplier are not just the purchasing department. The accounts people will need to be sure that payment terms and prices are fair, so that there is no unfavourable movement in cash flow, for instance. Production departments need to understand the differences between this component and the previous one; sales need to understand if this makes any difference to their methods or to the key selling points; marketing need to know if the current marketing strategy needs to change; human resources need to know if there are any issues of training or varying staff requirements occasioned by the change; shipping need to know about the way the components will arrive. The list will usually cover the entire company.

As we have seen, a meeting of all the heads of the departments involved to settle all the issues in one go will not work. If any department has reservations, they will be unlikely to voice them in public for fear of causing somebody else to lose face. So the discussions with each department have to be done individually. Normally, the department taking the lead in the decision (in the case of our widgets, the purchasing department) will conduct a series of discussions with each department in turn, investigating all the issues and trying to resolve individual difficulties. At this stage, questions may come back to you for resolution. They may be trivial, such as 'Can you pack widgets in tens rather than dozens?' or they may be more fundamental, such as 'Can you lower the price by ten per cent?' It is important that you do your best to answer all these questions openly and efficiently, because as long as the questions are still being asked, you are still in business. When the questions dry up, the project has most likely gone dead.

Public face and true intentions
You will also have to put into practice all you have discovered about the *tatemae* (建前) and the *honne* (本音), the public face and the true intentions. The Japanese never want to say no, so will always be looking for a way out of the negotiations if things are not developing in the way they had hoped. The most common

way, apart from just going silent on you, is to ask questions or make suggestions that they know will be unacceptable to you. If you only supply your widgets in blue or red, they will ask for green widgets, hoping that you will break off the talks because you cannot supply green ones. The real reason why they do not want to complete the negotiations will almost certainly be very different. Similarly, they may ask questions in such a way that they are really hoping you will see their point of view, because they really want to do the business (their *honne* position), but there is some internal reason why face must be maintained (the *tatemae* position).

Difficult questions

One aspect of the negotiation process that is usually very different from the western experience is that the Japanese like to set aside difficult questions and come back to them later, while we in the West tend to want to take the tough questions first, because if they cannot be settled, then there is little point in wasting time reaching agreement on the minor points. The Japanese style of negotiation comes partly from a desire to avoid confrontation, but also from a desire never to be the ones who say 'no'. If the issue is something they cannot agree to, they will put it to one side in the hope either that time will resolve it or that, if it is truly a stumbling block, something else will crop up during later negotiations which will be unacceptable to the other side, who will then be forced to be the ones to break off the deal. Be aware of this tendency and do not assume that because they have stopped talking about an issue, it is resolved. The opposite is more likely to be the case.

Making the decision

When eventually the questions are all resolved, things will move very quickly. There is no time frame for the whole *nemawashi* process, and this is why so many Westerners describe the Japanese decision-making process as incomprehensible and interminable. In fact, if you are keeping a close eye on how things are developing, by judiciously timed e-mails, phone calls and visits, you should be able to tell how near to a decision your Japanese partners are getting. It is only those companies who let the Japanese get on with the process, without making any other efforts to keep the relationship alive, who are sometimes surprised by the timing and outcome of the negotiation process.

RINGI

The way the Japanese announce a decision is by means of a document called the *ringi* (稟議 = 'circular memorandum'). As one commentator put it, 'corporate decisions and actions seldom take place without *ringi*'. Nor do government decisions and actions: Japanese bureaucrats use the *ringi* as a matter of routine. How does this document work? The *ringi* (or *ringi-sho*, '*sho*' merely means 'piece of paper') is an internal document which summarises the proposal and which is then circulated internally. It is usually brief and to the point, so that in the case of your widgets it would probably merely list in a series of bullet points the fact that the company was proposing to buy widgets from The Widget Corporation, in stated quantities at a stated price. It would list matters such as payment details, any staffing or training implications and quite possibly the names of the main contacts in the Widget Corporation. The memo would be generated by the department that originated the proposal, in this case purchasing, and would be circulated to every part of the company affected by the decision.

As the *ringi* reaches each department in turn, the department may well hold a brief meeting to confirm they are all happy with the contents (which have, of course, already been sorted out by the long-winded *nemawashi* process), and then the head of the department will place his seal on the document. The department chief's seal on the *ringi* is the sign that his team approves the document. It then passes on to the next department where the process is repeated. When the *ringi* has returned to its originator with all the seals imprinted on the paper, the decision is made. The first you may hear about it, however, may well be the placing of a first order. Unless you keep your relationship contacts strong, you may not be aware how close to a decision your Japanese colleagues have got.

It is worth remembering that if you do not keep in close contact with Japanese firms while the consensus gathering process is going on, you may well be surprised by the speed of events once the decision is made. You have to keep them fully informed of any development on your side that may affect the final deal. In the case of our widgets, they will want to place an order on the terms and conditions already offered, so it is no good going back to them once the order is placed and saying that the specification has changed or the price has gone up, or the factory is on holiday for a week. You should have kept them informed of all these issues, even if there appeared to be no movement on their side. You cannot see a Japanese decision being made, but the *nemawashi* process is going on all the time.

DECISIVENESS IS A SIN

Japanese decisions are group decisions. This gives them one major disadvantage in our eyes, but one major advantage. The major disadvantage is that they take a long time. Decisiveness is a sin in Japan, because it implies you are not consulting with others when you take a decision, but consultation takes time. In the West, time is money, and we cannot waste time checking that everybody in the organisation is happy with every decision. We'd never get anything done.

The Japanese, on the other hand, need unanimity. In actual fact, it is highly unlikely that any decision is unanimous, even in Japan, but the *nemawashi* process allows those who oppose an idea to adjust their *tatemae*, their official position, to that of the wishes of the group, even if their *honne* is that they feel the whole idea is daft. In the West, we would let our colleagues know what we really feel about a business project, because we feel it is important not to compromise our own personal beliefs, but in Japan the group is more important than the individual. The decision of the majority quickly becomes unanimous.

There is a risk that some of the decisions reached by consensus are somewhat anodyne, being merely the least unacceptable of the options put forward. In practice, this is rarely the case in Japan, because people are very quickly sensitive to the needs of the group, and allow bold decisions to be agreed if that is the mood of the organisation. The advantage of this method of making decisions is that everybody, at least in their *tatemae*, agrees with the decision, so that it can be enacted quickly and effectively. Too often in Western business, decisions can be made very quickly, but as they are put into effect, opposition begins to arise. This may be because the sort of discussions that the Japanese had before the decision was finalised are only now for the first time being aired.

Making quick western-style decisions is pointless if they are never acted upon.

THE LEGAL POSITION

We have already noted that the Japanese consider lawyers largely unnecessary. All the same, they use the law to bind their business agreements just as we do. The difference is that in the legal department of a major Japanese corporation, you will probably find no more than one fully qualified lawyer, if that. Japanese legal departments are full of people who know exactly how effective their contracts have been over the years, which clauses work and which do not, what has to be stated and how to skate gently over the contentious issues and leave it suitably imprecise when imprecision is called for.

They are also full of people whose previous experience has been with the company's production departments, or out on the road selling, or working out pay scales within human resources, so they have a practical experience of the impact of the agreements they are working on that is probably far greater than their western counterparts. Japanese legal departments are made up of specialists in the minutiae of their company's legal and practical needs, so they are a formidable force.

Attitude to contracts

When an agreement is concluded, more often than not the contract is placed on file somewhere, and is never consulted again. In the rapidly changing world of Japanese business, where international habits are becoming more general throughout Japan, the attitude towards legal documentation is changing, but on the whole, the Japanese see a contract merely as a symbol of the business relationship it describes. It is not something that needs to be looked at, unless the business is going radically wrong.

In the West, we tend to consult contracts much more often, and use them as a template for how the business should be run: but not in Japan. Contracts are to satisfy the other party, but the business is conducted on the basis of ever closer personal and corporate relationships, which do not need a piece of paper to turn them into reality. That is not to say that the terms of a contract are flouted – they are not. It is merely not the Japanese custom to worry whether every sub-clause of every agreement is being carefully adhered to, provided that the business defined by the contract is proceeding satisfactorily for both parties.

YOUR AGENDA OR MINE

The concept of 'satisfactorily for both parties' is another that can often lead to misunderstandings. It goes without saying that when one does a deal within one's own culture, there is an assumption that the other party has his or her own agenda, which does not necessarily coincide in all aspects with one's own. This is understood and allowed for. The pursuit of different agendas by partners in business does not often lead to the breakdown of the business altogether.

It ought to go without saying that two business partners based in different countries, even if they are contemplating full merger or a joint venture, will have different concepts of what the business should be doing, and how to define success or failure. In my experience, too many western business people have come to Japan somehow believing that their purpose in doing business there is transparent (to them, at least) so the motivation of the Japanese side should be transparent too.

We have already seen, however, that the Japanese are very good at separating their public face from their real intentions. They will, to be polite to the visitor, profess a set of targets or goals for their mutual business that coincides with his. To the extent that the Japanese truly always look for a win/win situation in their business arrangements, this will be the truth, but it would be naïve to assume that a Japanese company's reasons for working with a western company are the same as their partner's. Their agenda is indeed hidden, because it would be impolite and potentially confrontational to reveal it, but it is there to be found, and it is always worth looking for it.

Different goals can easily be reconciled, but only if they are recognised as different from the outset. The Japanese person will know your agenda, because you will have told him. You will not necessarily know his, because he will not wish to upset the agreement by professing to different hopes and aims for the business. Find it out.

9

Experiencing Japan

Japan is definitely a foreign country. To be effective in business in Japan, you also have to feel a little at home in the country. If you are merely going to be a visitor to Japan, however frequently, you will be unlikely to fit into the fabric of daily life in the way that a resident can do, and there is no doubt that even staying in a plush western hotel in Tokyo, you can feel entirely alien. Just watch the 2003 film *Lost In Translation* for a wry look at being a foreigner in today's Tokyo. But that should not prevent even a first time visitor from trying to get to know the sights, sounds, tastes and smells of Japan, to learn a little of what interests and excites the Japanese, and what just does not happen there.

HARMONY AND THE GROUP

In trying to analyse the essence of Japan (if there is such a thing: even in such a homogenous society, there is no 'typical' Japanese), we always come back to the idea of the group and the relationship between people. Japanese society is a long search for *wa*, a desire to find harmony in everything and in every action. Bowing to the needs of the group before satisfying one's own desires makes for a very different way of going about one's daily life, and it shows in the way that Japanese society works.

To take a simple example, the way that Japanese people like to spend their leisure time is almost as regulated as the way they spend their time at work. There are times when it is appropriate to go to the beach and times when it is not. This may have nothing to do with the weather, just with custom. In the same way that schoolchildren all change from winter to summer clothing on the same day, regardless of the outside temperature, so the beaches all empty at the beginning of September, because September is not part of the sea bathing season in Japan. Early September may enjoy some of the hottest days of the summer, but the beaches will be empty. Japan works because in general everybody knows what behaviour is appropriate under different circumstances. If you try to go against the grain too much, you will remain *soto*.

LEISURE TIME

All this can create huge pressures on the individual. As people who have to suppress their true feelings practically all the time, their leisure time is carefully guarded. Leisure time does not include time spent with the family, as it would in the West. Free time spent by a working father at weekends with the family is known as 'family service', which has overtones of community service and shows how eagerly the average Japanese Dad takes part in family activities such as shopping or weekend outings. Any moments that can be spent outside the bounds of social obligations are gratefully snatched. In a society where the interests of the group are paramount, the most popular leisure activities are solitary ones. They can be divided into two main sections: sports and alcohol.

In Japan, the most popular spectator sports are baseball and horseracing. The Japanese are inveterate gamblers, not to the extent of the Chinese perhaps, but they enjoy a bet. Japanese betting is, however, far better regulated than in many societies, and although they bet heavily on the horses, on speedboat racing and cycle racing among others, they tend to watch team sports such as baseball without having the urge to bet on every pitch and every inning.

PINBALL WIZARDS

One of the most popular gambling pastimes is the pinball game *pachinko*. *Pachinko* parlours (the name is onomatopoeic, imitating the sound of the metal ball as it clunks around the machine) are everywhere in Japan, and they consume a surprisingly large percentage of the entire GDP of Japan. You will see *pachinko* halls in every neighbourhood, full of housewives, businessmen in dark suits, labourers who have just left a building site, and even junior gangsters in sharp three piece suits and pointed leather shoes. Everybody plays *pachinko*. They stand there entranced, staring at the machine while they feed the balls in with one hand and flip the flipper with the other. No other muscle moves.

It is not officially somewhere you can gamble: you buy a tray of metal balls and play them until they are all used up, or until you decide to cash in your remaining *pachinko* balls. The machines themselves do not give out money or prizes, only more metal balls, and you cannot cash in your balls for money, only for prizes. However, there are shops down the street which specialise in buying back *pachinko* prizes, so a lucky winner can take his cigarettes, dried noodles or travelling alarm clock to one of these establishments and sell them for cash. It is a complicated way to get round a law, but it keeps a lot of people in work.

Most people, especially those who play *pachinko* only rarely, use the parlours as a cheap way of passing an hour or two, but there are *pachinko* professionals who make a living out of playing the game. These are the people who play all day every day, and quickly learn which machines are paying out more than others (every pachinko parlour has a machine or two that is more generous than others, to keep the punters interested, and the position of these machines is changed very regularly). By monopolising one of these big paying machines, they can make a bit of money.

Pachinko does not, as far as I know, have championships or a national champion, because it is a purely individual pastime. *Pachinko* players can switch off from the world around them, and find a little personal space within an overcrowded city.

SPORTS

Team sports, such as baseball, football and rugby, are very popular in Japan (as the 2002 Football World Cup in Japan and Korea proved), but in participation terms they fall a long way behind activities like golf, fishing and the martial arts such as judo and kendo. Tennis, cycling and walking are other popular pastimes, and the link between all of these activities is that they are not essentially communal sports.

You may play golf with other people, or compete against somebody else in judo, but the essence of all these activities, especially the native Japanese sports, is that they pit the participant against themselves, not against another person. Judo, kendo and even sumo wrestling are about inner strength, inner concentration and the perfection of technique. The opponent is irrelevant. Golf is a battle between the individual and the golf course, while fishing gives every angler the chance to sit alone and in silence by a river or a canal, probably hoping that no fish will actually be so foolish as to accept the bait on the end of his hook. The Japanese angler has found peace without obligation, which is possibly the main reason why it is such a popular pastime.

There are two ways of shaking off the shackles of social obligation. The first way is to shake off the rest of society, by going fishing or becoming a *judoka*. The second way is to ignore the shackles themselves, to find a way of ignoring the rules of Japanese society. The most obvious way of doing this is to get drunk.

DRINKING TO FORGET

The role of alcohol in Japanese society is unusual.

Sake

Sake (酒 = rice wine) has been a part of Japanese society since at least the eighth century AD. It is a clear liquid distilled from rice, with an alcoholic strength of between 16% and 18%, traditionally drunk warm in small porcelain cups called *sakazuki*. These days it is also marketed as a chilled drink, drunk with ice in the same way that sherry has been rebranded as a modern drink if you drop a couple of ice cubes in the glass.

Beer

Sake is not the only alcoholic drink available in Japan, and these days is not even the most widely consumed. Beer is hugely popular, with three major brands, Kirin, Asahi and Sapporo, dominating the local market and nowadays proving very successful in many overseas markets. They are mainly of a lager type, although darker beers are also popular.

Whisky

Whisky is also a very popular drink, with local brands Suntory and Nikka holding the biggest market shares. Scotch whisky still has a tremendous cachet, commanding far higher prices than the local whisky, as do American brands such as Jack Daniels. Scotch whisky, which is still one of Britain's major exports to Japan, used to be the subject of heated negotiations during the 1960s and 1970s when there was a fixed import quota on Scotch whisky, aimed at protecting the local industry. Suntory is now deemed to be strong enough to look after itself, and there are no longer any import quotas in place for Scotch or any other alcoholic drink.

Losing your inhibitions

The reason why alcohol is so much a part of the fabric of Japanese life, apart from the obvious personal reasons of taste and its after effects which apply in any culture, is that it has always been Japanese custom to ignore anything that a person does under the influence of drink. All behaviour can be excused if one has had too much to drink. So the Japanese love to get drunk. It is said that there is something in the Japanese metabolism that makes them more prone to the effects of alcohol than Europeans. Certainly the fact that until recently the average Japanese was smaller than the average Westerner meant that a smaller amount of alcohol would produce an equally devastating effect, but all the same it is surprising to see Japanese businessmen going red in the face after only a glass or two of beer and suddenly throwing off their inhibitions.

But if you lived in a society where every move, every thought, every emotion was governed by the need to fit in with others, you would also be looking for ways to shake off this burden of unbearable harmony every now and again. Alcohol affords this release. I have known junior business people get drunk in a bar and insult their superiors, I have seen people throwing up over their office colleagues as they leave a bar late at night, but providing that the offenders turn up sober and bright-eyed at work the next morning, all will be forgotten. He was drunk, so his behaviour did not count.

It was even the case in the early post-war years that drink driving was not a crime: indeed, a driver could use as his defence the fact that he was drunk at the time and therefore not responsible for his own actions. Those days, incidentally, are long gone. The legal maximum permitted for alcohol in the blood of a driver today is 0 ppm. Under no circumstances in Japan contemplate drinking and driving.

KARAOKE

When the Japanese drink, they also enjoy *karaoke*. There seem to be two types of karaoke performer in Japan – the extraordinarily brilliant and the truly awful. There is no middle ground. However, karaoke is something that everybody takes part in, and the only crime in Japan is not being willing to join in and sing. It does not matter how bad a singer you are, you can guarantee not only that there will be somebody even worse than you performing before the night is out, but also that your efforts will be rewarded with a huge round of applause from everybody in the bar. So go ahead and do it.

Nobody you care about need hear your version of 'My Way'. Neither Bjorn or Benny from Abba are likely to be listening to your version of 'Mamma Mia'. But there will be plenty of

Japanese wanting you to have a go, and the worst insult you can give them is to refuse to join in. I remember an Australian visitor who claimed in a karaoke bar not even to know the words to 'Waltzing Matilda'. While the rest of the people in the bar – Japanese, Brits, Chinese, Greeks and Brazilians – all gathered around the machine singing about billabongs and jumbucks, the Australian sat on his chair staring stonily into his beer. The result was that the Japanese thereafter did not give a XXXX for that particular Australian, and all chances were gone of his doing business with anybody who had seen him that night.

THE JAPANESE WAY

In Japan there are no hard and fast rules. Equally one can say that there is no great secret about the way that the Japanese do business, or the way they manage their staff. It is all a matter of common sense. If you treat your employees as human beings, as an integral part of the relationships that make up a company, then they are more likely to work well and stick around longer. It is the difference between the analogue and the digital, between the team and the individual. The Japanese would claim that their approach gives each individual respect, and that the western approach treats people like machines. In Japan, respect is granted to the team player, while in the West it is bestowed for individual achievement.

Trust

One western executive on the board of a joint venture in Japan said that his Japanese partners had said to them, 'You need to walk into the mist.' In his view, that meant that the partners had to have faith in each other, and not to worry about what could go wrong. If there is that basic trust within the relationship, the

Japanese believe it will work. Faith and trust are two things that anybody can provide: you do not have to be a specialist in Japan to have trust in your business partners.

Behind the mask

If you are sensitive to the Japanese way of doing business, and if you take an interest in the Japanese way of life, you will be accepted. If the business model is workable, you will succeed. If you can begin to accept the Japanese mask as an alternative reality, and that what is behind the Japanese mask is just as unreal as the mask itself, then you have started to understand that Japan is probably incomprehensible.

The masks used by the actors in the traditional Japanese Noh dramas can appear happy or sad, depending on how you look at them. In different lights a Noh mask expresses comedy or tragedy, and the actors are experts in exploiting the light to give the impression they want. As one American put it, 'The question "Is she a beautiful woman or not?" depends on the opinion of who is looking at her. Is all Japan a conspiracy? It depends on how you look at it.'

DON'T BE SURPRISED

When I first came to work in Japan, I arrived armed with one piece of advice. My father, who spent many years working in Japan and the Far East in the first 20 years after the war, said to me just before I flew out of Heathrow, 'When you get to Japan, just remember one thing.' He paused and I thought that this was a pivotal moment in our relationship: my dad was handing on the wisdom of his generation to the young pretender. 'Just one thing. Don't be surprised.'

I have to say that as wisdoms of generations go, this did not seem to me to be from the top drawer. Was that all there was to it? Don't be surprised? But as time passed and I tried to come to terms with Japan and its business and culture, I began to understand that Dad was not such a fool after all. Surprise is the gap between what we expect and what we get. If we are expecting a handshake and we get a custard pie in the face, we are surprised. If we are expecting the custard pie, there is no surprise.

What my father was saying to me was that in a culture where you do not know the rules, you will always be surprised if you persist in assuming that the way you are used to things being done is the only way things ought to happen. If, however, you drop all the preconceived ideas, if you take things purely at face value, then you will not be surprised. You will have a chance to judge the things you see and the things that happen to you on their own merit, and not in western terms. You will not be able to change things to any extent, so why try? Understand how the Japanese do things, even if you do not always understand why.

Memory clear

If you refuse to be surprised, then everything becomes logical on its own terms. It's like using a pocket calculator (incidentally one of the inventions that did surprise me when Casio brought out the first tiny calculator in the early 1970s). Before you start a new calculation, you have to press the Memory Clear button, or else you are in danger of getting the wrong answer. If you do not press the Memory Clear button in your mind, if you prejudge Japan by what you have experienced elsewhere, you will too often come up with the wrong answers. Press the Memory Clear button in your mind, and you might not always understand the answer, but with any luck you won't be surprised.

Hiragana and Katakana: the Japanese Phonetic Syllabaries

HIRAGANA

	k	s	t	n	h	m	y	r	w	−n
a	あ	か	さ	た	な	は	ま	や	ら	わ	ん
i	い	き	し	ち	に	ひ	み		り		
u	う	く	す	つ	ぬ	ふ	む	ゆ	る		
e	え	け	せ	て	ね	へ	め		れ		
o	お	こ	そ	と	の	ほ	も	よ	ろ	を	

KATAKANA

	k	s	t	n	h	m	y	r	w	−n
a	ア	カ	サ	タ	ナ	ハ	マ	ヤ	ラ	ワ	ン
i	イ	キ	シ	チ	ニ	ヒ	ミ		リ		
u	ウ	ク	ス	ツ	ヌ	フ	ム	ユ	ル		
e	エ	ケ	セ	テ	ネ	ヘ	メ		レ		
o	オ	コ	ソ	ト	ノ	ホ	モ	ヨ	ロ	ヲ	

Softening of consonants is produced by adding a diacritical mark to the top right hand corner of the kana: か (ka) becomes が (ga), for example. To make the plosive 'p' sound, a diacritical mark is added to the 'h' kana, so that へ (he) becomes ぺ (pe), for example.

Western names are transliterated in katakana. So Tony Blair would become トウニ ブレアー (Tounii Bureaa) and Jonathan Rice would become ジョナサン　ライス (Jiyonasan Raisu). Some names become very complicated to decipher.

Bibliography

Some suggested further reference materials – books, websites and films.

BOOKS

Non-fiction:

British Envoys in Japan 1859-1972, ed. Hugh Cortazzi (Japan Society, 2004)

Building Cross-cultural Competence, Fons Trompenaars and Charles Hampden-Turner (John Wiley, 2000)

The Cambridge Encyclopaedia of Japan, ed. Richard Bowring and Peter Kornicki (Cambridge University Press, 1993)

Charting Japanese Industry, Tomokazu Ohsono (Cassell, 1995)

The Chrysanthemum and the Sword, Ruth Benedict (Tuttle, 1946)

Cultures and Organizations, Geert Hofstede (Harper Collins, 1994)

Doing Business in Japan, Jonathan Rice (BBC 1992)

Embracing Defeat, John Dower (Penguin, 2000)

Encyclopaedia of Japanese Pop Culture, Mark Schilling (Tuttle, 1997)

Guide to Reading and Writing Japanese, ed. Florence Sakade (Tuttle, 1959)

The Inscrutable Japanese, Hiroshi Kagawa (Kodansha, 1997)

Inventing Japan, Ian Buruma (Weidenfeld & Nicolson, 2003)

Japan, A History in Art, Bradley Smith (Doubleday, 1964)

The Japanese, Edwin O. Reischauer (Tuttle, 1977)

The Japanese Achievement, Hugh Cortazzi (Sidgwick & Jackson, 1990)

Japanese Business Language, an Essential Dictionary (KPI, 1987)

Japanese Etiquette and Ethics in Business, Boye de Mente (Phoenix, 1987)

The Mind of the Strategist, Kenichi Ohmae (Penguin, 1983)

The Modern Reader's Japanese. English Character Dictionary. Andrew Nelson (Tuttle, 1962)

Nippon, New Superpower, William Horsley and Roger Buckley (BBC, 1990)

The Nobility of Failure, Ivan Morris (Tuttle, 1975)

Sources of Japanese Tradition, ed. Wm. Theodore de Bary, (Columbia University Press, 1964)

Fiction

An Artist of the Floating World, Kazuo Ishiguro (Faber & Faber, 1986)

Confessions of a Mask, Yukio Mishimo (Tuttle, 1970)

Dance Dance Dance, Haruki Murakami (Panther, 2002)

A Death in Tokyo, Guy Stanley (Michael Joseph, 1988)

The Makioka Sisters, Junichiro Tanizaki (Tuttle, 1957)

Memoirs of a Geisha, Arthur Golden (Vintage Books, 1998)

Norwegian Wood, Haruki Murakami (Panther, 2001)

Number 9 Dream, David Mitchell (Sceptre, 2001)

The Sumurai, Shunsaka Endo (Penguin, 1983)

WEBSITES

www.japantimes.co.jp	The main English language newspaper in Tokyo
www.japan-guide.co.jp	A good general tourist guide to Japan
www.meti.go.jp	The Ministry of the Economy, Trade and Industry
www.mofa.go.jp	The Ministry of Foreign Affairs

FILMS

The Last Samurai (USA, 2003)

Lost in Translation (USA, 2003)
Ran (乱) (Japan, 1985)
Rashomon (羅生門) (Japan, 1950)
The Seven Samurai (七人の侍) (Japan, 1954)
Tokyo Story (東京物語り) (Japan, 1953)
Ugetsu Monogatari (雨月物語り) (Japan, 1953)
Woman of the Dunes (砂の女) (Japan, 1964)

With the exception of the first – a Tom Cruise vehicle which
nevertheless works – the others are classic films dealing with
Japanese-ness.

Index